P9-AOZ-055

Pre-GED Connection™

Language Arts, Writing

by Karin Evans and Ellen Frechette

LiteracyLink® is a joint project of PBS,
Kentucky Educational Television,
the National Center on Adult Literacy,
and the Kentucky Department of Education.

This project is funded in whole,
or in part, by the Star Schools Program
of the USDE under contract #R203D60001.

 **PBS** LiteracyLink®

 KET

NCAL

Acknowledgments

LiteracyLink® Advisory Board

Lynn Allen, Idaho Public Television
Anthony Buttino, WNED-TV
Anthony Carnevale, Educational
    Testing Service
Andy Chaves, Marriott International, Inc.
Patricia Edwards, Michigan State University
Phyllis Eisen, Center for Workforce Success National
    Association of Manufacturers
Maggi Gaines, Baltimore Reads, Inc.
Marshall Goldberg, Association of Joint Labor
    Management Educational Programs
Milton Goldberg, National Alliance
    for Business
Neal Johnson, Association of Governing Boards of
    Universities and Colleges
Cynthia Johnston, Central Piedmont Community
    College
Sandra Kestner, Kentucky Department for Adult
    Education and Literacy
Thomas Kinney, American Association of Adult and
    Continuing Education
Dale Lipschultz, American Library Association
Lennox McLendon, National Adult Education
    Professional Development Consortium
Cam Messina, KLRN
Patricia Miller, KNPB
Cathy Powers, WLRN
Ray Ramirez, U.S. Department of Education
Emma Rhodes, (retired) Arkansas Department of
    Education
Cynthia Ruiz, KCET
Tony Sarmiento, Worker Centered Learning,
    Working for America Institute
Steve Steurer, Correctional
    Education Association
LaShell Stevens-Staley, Iowa PTV
Fran Tracy-Mumford, Delaware Department of
    Adult/Community Education
Terilyn Turner, Community Education,
    St. Paul Public Schools

LiteracyLink® Ex Officio Advisory Board

Joan Auchter, GED Testing Service
Barbara Derwart, U.S. Department of Labor
Cheryl Garnette, OERI, U.S.
    Department of Education
Andrew Hartman, National Institute
    for Literacy
Mary Lovell, OVAE, U.S. Department
    of Education
Ronald Pugsley, OVAE, U.S. Department
    of Education
Linda Roberts, U.S. Department of Education
Joe Wilkes, OERI, U.S. Department of Education

LiteracyLink® Partners

LiteracyLink® is a joint project of:
    Public Broadcasting Service,
    Kentucky Educational Television,
    National Center on Adult Literacy, and the
    Kentucky Department of Education.

Content Design and Workbook Editorial Development

    Learning Unlimited, Oak Park, Illinois

Design and Layout

    By Design, Lexington, Kentucky

Project Coordinators

    Milli Fazey, KET, Lexington, Kentucky
    Margaret Norman, KET, Lexington, Kentucky

This project is funded in whole, or in part, by the
Star Schools Program of the USDE under contract
#R203D60001.

PBS LiteracyLink® is a registered mark of the
Public Broadcasting Service.

No part of this book may be reproduced or transmitted in
any form or by any means, electronic or mechanical,
including photocopying, recording, or by any information
storage and retrieval without permission in writing from
the publisher.

The editor has made every effort to trace the ownership of
all copyrighted material, and necessary permissions have
been secured in most cases. Should there prove to be any
question regarding the use of any material, regret is here
expressed for such error. Upon notification of any such
oversight, proper acknowledgment will be made in future
editions.

Copyright © 2003, KET. Reprinted 2007. All rights reserved.

Printed in the United States of America.
ISBN # 1-881020-49-5
ISBN # 978-1-881020-49-3

Contents

Introduction

Welcome to *Pre-GED Language Arts, Writing*. This workbook is part of the *LiteracyLink®* multimedia educational system for adult learners and educators. The system includes *Pre-GED Connection*, which builds a foundation for GED-level study and *GED Connection*, which learners use to study for the GED Tests. *LiteracyLink* also includes *Workplace Essential Skills*, which targets upgrading the knowledge and skills needed to succeed in the world of work.

Pre-GED CONNECTION consists of these educational tools:

26 VIDEO PROGRAMS shown on public television and in adult learning centers

ONLINE MATERIALS available on the Internet at http://www.pbs.org/literacy

FIVE Pre-GED COMPANION WORKBOOKS

Language Arts, Writing
Language Arts, Reading
Social Studies
Science
Mathematics

Instructional Programs

Pre-GED Connection consists of 26 instructional video programs and five companion workbooks. Each *Pre-GED Connection* workbook lesson accompanies a video program. For example, the first lesson in this book is *Program 1— Getting Ideas on Paper*. This workbook lesson should be used with *Pre-GED Connection Video Program 1—Getting Ideas on Paper*. In addition, you can go online to www.pbs.org/literacy and click the *Pre-GED Writing* link.

Who's Responsible for LiteracyLink®?

LiteracyLink was developed through a five-year grant by the U.S. Department of Education. The following partners have contributed to the development of the *LiteracyLink* system:

PBS Adult Learning Service

Kentucky Educational Television (KET)

The National Center on Adult Literacy (NCAL) of the University of Pennsylvania

The Kentucky Department of Education

All of the *LiteracyLink* partners wish you the very best in meeting all of your educational goals.

Getting Started with *Pre-GED Connection Language Arts, Writing*

Before you start using the workbook, take some time to preview its features.

1. Take the **Pretest** on page 6. This will help you decide which areas you need to focus on. You should use the evaluation chart on page 19 to develop your study plan.

2. Work through the **workbook lessons**—each one corresponds to a video program.

   The *Before You Watch* feature sets up the video program:
   - **Think About the Topic** gives a brief overview of the video
   - **Prepare to Watch the Video** is a short activity with instant feedback that shows how everyday knowledge can help you better understand the topic
   - **Lesson Goals** highlight the main ideas of each video and workbook lesson
   - **Terms** introduces key writing vocabulary

   The *After You Watch* feature helps you evaluate what you saw:

   - **Think About the Program** presents questions that focus on key points from the video
   - **Make the Connection** applies what you have learned to real-life situations

   Three *Writing Skills* sections correspond to key concepts in the video program. Extra practice for skills in this section starts on page 140.

   The *Writer's Tool* sections provide you with techniques and exercises to improve your writing habits and skills and to help you succeed on both sections of the GED Writing Test. Program 2 introduces you to the portfolio that you will use throughout this book.

   The *GED Essay Connection* sections offer sample essay topics and activities.

   GED Practice allows you to practice with the types of problems that you will see on the actual test.

3. Take the **Posttest** on page 164 to determine your progress and whether you are ready for GED-level work.

4. Use the **Answer Key** to check your answers.

5. Refer to the **Writing Handbook** at the back of the book as needed.

For Teachers

Portions of *LiteracyLink* have been developed for adult educators and service providers. Teachers can use Pre-GED lesson plans in the *LiteracyLink Teacher's Guide* binder. This binder also contains lesson plans for *GED Connection* and *Workplace Essential Skills*.

Writing Pretest

Part 1: Sample Test Item

This pretest will help you find out how much you already know. The questions in this first part are like those on the GED Language Arts, Writing Test. This part has 19 questions based on passages of real-life writing, just like the GED Test.

Here's a sample question. Read the sentence in **bold** type. Does it contain an error? If so, which answer choice is the best way to correct the error?

We are determined not to get sick this <u>winter, we</u> are all getting flu shots.

Which is the best way to write the underlined portion of this sentence?
If the original is the best way, choose option (1).

(1) winter, we
(2) winter we
(3) winter and we
(4) winter, so we
(5) winter so we

Look at the answer sheet sample, then go over the explanation of why the correct answer is correct. Then read the explanation below.

Did you notice that the original sentence is not punctuated correctly? It has two complete thoughts joined only by a comma. There is usually more than one way to fix an error like that. However, there will be only one correct answer choice for each test question. Your job is to figure out which answer choice makes the sentence correct.

You can eliminate choice 1 because the original sentence is wrong. You can also eliminate choice 2 because it would run two complete thoughts together with no punctuation. Choices 3 and 5 are incorrect also. Each has a needed connecting word (*and* or *so*) but no comma. **Choice 4** is correct because it has a comma *and* a connecting word.

Some sentences in test items are correct. If you think there is no error in a sentence or paragraph, you may be right. Some questions, such as the one above, say, "If the original is the best way, choose option (1)." Another type of question gives you this option: (5) "no correction is necessary." Look at all the answer choices before you decide.

As you answer the questions, fill in numbers 1 through 19 on the grid on page 7. Then go on to the next part of the pretest, beginning on page 14.

Writing Pretest

Part 1: Directions

1. Read the sample test item on page 6 to become familiar with the test format.

2. Take the test on pages 8 through 17. Read each passage, and then choose the best answer to each question.

3. Record your answers on the answer sheet below, using a No. 2 pencil.

4. Check your work against the Answers and Explanations on page 18.

5. Enter your scores in the evaluation chart on page 19.

WRITING PRETEST ■ ANSWER SHEET

Name _____   Date _____

Class _____

1. ①②③④⑤	6. ①②③④⑤	11. ①②③④⑤	16. ①②③④⑤	21. ①②③④⑤
2. ①②③④⑤	7. ①②③④⑤	12. ①②③④⑤	17. ①②③④⑤	22. ①②③④⑤
3. ①②③④⑤	8. ①②③④⑤	13. ①②③④⑤	18. ①②③④⑤	23. ①②③④⑤
4. ①②③④⑤	9. ①②③④⑤	14. ①②③④⑤	19. ①②③④⑤	24. ①②③④⑤
5. ①②③④⑤	10. ①②③④⑤	15. ①②③④⑤	20. ①②③④⑤	25. ①②③④⑤

Choose the <u>one best answer</u> to each question.

<u>Questions 1 through 6</u> refer to the following business letter.

Ms. Elena Ortiz
South Wind Motel
321 Lakeside Boulevard
Hampton, SC 29924

Dear Ms. Ortiz:

(A)

(1) As you requested, I am putting my complaint in writing. (2) If we work together we can resolve this problem. (3) You want to maintain the good reputation of your business, I certainly want to be known as an honest customer.

(B)

(4) As I stated on the phone, I called the South Wind Motel back in May. (5) I made a reservation for a room with your desk clerk he asked for my credit card number. (6) He also assured me that I would not be charged if I canceled the reservation at least 48 hours in advance. (7) I marked August 8 on my calendar. (8) Because my reservation was for August 10. (9) As your records show, Ms. Ortiz, my wife and I did not stay at your motel that night. (10) I did in fact call to cancel our reservation at South Wind on August 8.

(C)

(11) I spoke with the night manager. (12) I told her we would not be staying that night. (13) I assumed that this effectively cancelled my reservation. (14) However, my last credit card bill shows a charge of $89.00 from the South Wind and I would like this charge taken off my bill. (15) Ms. Ortiz, please address this issue and get back to me as soon as possible.

Sincerely,

Mr. Samuel Franklin

1. Sentence 2: **If we work <u>together we</u> can resolve this problem.**

   Which is the best way to write the underlined portion of this sentence? If the original is the best way, choose option (1).
   (1) together we
   (2) together. We
   (3) together then we
   (4) together, and we
   (5) together, we

2. Sentence 3: **You want to maintain the good reputation of your business, I certainly want to be known as an honest customer.**

   Which correction should be made to sentence 3?
   (1) change <u>You want</u> to <u>You wanting</u>
   (2) insert a comma after <u>reputation</u>
   (3) remove the comma after <u>business</u>
   (4) insert <u>and</u> after the comma
   (5) no correction is necessary

3. Sentence 5: **I made a reservation for a room with your desk <u>clerk he</u> asked for my credit card number.**

Which is the best way to write the underlined portion of this sentence? If the original is the best way, choose option (1).
(1) clerk he
(2) clerk. He
(3) clerk, he
(4) clerk and he
(5) clerk so he

4. Sentences 7 and 8: **I marked August 8 on my <u>calendar. Because</u> my reservation was for August 10.**

Which is the best way to write the underlined portion of these sentences? If the original is the best way, choose option (1).
(1) calendar. Because
(2) calendar and because
(3) calendar because
(4) calendar, even though
(5) calendar, but

5. Sentences 11 and 12: **I spoke with the night manager. I told her we would not be staying that night.**

The most effective combination of sentences 11 and 12 would include which group of words?
(1) spoke with the night manager and told her
(2) Telling the night manager
(3) When I told the night manager
(4) I spoke and told the night manager
(5) and speaking with the night manager

6. Sentence 14: **However, my last credit card bill shows a charge of $89.00 from the South Wind and I would like this charge taken off my bill.**

Which correction should be made to sentence 14?
(1) insert <u>because</u> after the comma
(2) change <u>shows</u> to <u>showing</u>
(3) insert a comma after <u>Wind</u>
(4) remove the word <u>and</u>
(5) no correction is necessary

Questions 7 through 13 refer to the following information.

Buy Food Wisely

(A)

(1) Food manufacturers work hard to get people to buy its products. (2) Therefore, consumers must be aware of the techniques used to influence their decision making. (3) Your goals might be to provide both healthful and reasonably priced food for you and your family. (4) However, don't assume that them are the goals of food companies. (5) Here is some marketing strategies that companies use to increase their profits at the expense of your health and wallet.

(B)

(6) Did you know that food of all kinds becomes more expensive as it is processed more? (7) Therefore, if a company can get you to buy frozen dinners instead of fresh fruits and vegetables, it will make more money. (8) To make processed food more appealing, companies create a huge variety of products and place them in colorful, attractive packaging.

(C)

(9) In addition, consider the layout of your grocery store. (10) Companies in the food industry pays to have their products displayed at eye level on store shelves. (11) Less expensive, more healthful products are shelved where you had to bend down or reach up to get them. (12) Also, have you ever wondered why milk, a popular food item, been stored way in the back of the store? (13) It's so you will pick up the potato chips and cookies you see on the way to the dairy case!

(D)

(14) Finally, think about all the food ads you see in magazines and on television. (15) Advertising influences people, and food companies spend billions of dollars a year to influence you to buy their products.

7. Sentence 1: **Food manufacturers work hard to get people to buy its products.**

   Which correction should be made to sentence 1?
   (1) change <u>work</u> to <u>working</u>
   (2) change <u>work</u> to <u>worked</u>
   (3) change <u>buy</u> to <u>be buying</u>
   (4) replace <u>its</u> with <u>their</u>
   (5) no correction is necessary

8. Sentence 4: **However, don't assume that them are the goals of food companies.**

   Which correction should be made to sentence 4?
   (1) remove the comma after <u>However</u>
   (2) change <u>assume</u> to <u>have assumed</u>
   (3) replace <u>them</u> with <u>they</u>
   (4) change <u>are</u> to <u>be</u>
   (5) no correction is necessary

9. Sentence 5: **Here <u>is</u> some marketing strategies that companies use to increase their profits at the expense of your health and wallet.**

   Which is the best way to write the underlined portion of this sentence? If the original is the best way, choose option (1).
   (1) is
   (2) are
   (3) was
   (4) be
   (5) were

10. Sentence 6: **Did you know that food of all kinds becomes more expensive as it is processed more?**

Which correction should be made to sentence 6?
(1) change becomes to became
(2) change becomes to become
(3) insert a comma after expensive
(4) replace it is with they are
(5) no correction is necessary

11. Sentence 10: **Companies in the food industry pays to have their products displayed at eye level on store shelves.**

Which correction should be made to sentence 10?
(1) insert a comma after industry
(2) insert they after industry
(3) change pays to pay
(4) replace their with its
(5) no correction is necessary

12. Sentence 11: **Less expensive, more healthful products are shelved where you had to bend down or reach up to get them.**

Which is the best way to write the underlined portion of this sentence? If the original is the best way, choose option (1).
(1) had
(2) have
(3) are having
(4) will have
(5) have had

13. Sentence 12: **Also, have you ever wondered why milk, a popular food item, been stored way in the back of the store?**

Which is the best way to write the underlined portion of this sentence? If the original is the best way, choose option (1).
(1) been
(2) being
(3) will be
(4) is being
(5) is

Questions 14 through 19 refer to the following information.

Family Histories

(A)

(1) Researching and recording you're family history can be a fun and rewarding adventure. (2) With some time and patience, you can preserve your family's stories forever. (3) What a gift to be past on to future generations! (4) While the task may seem daunting at first, you have lots of resources on which to draw.

(B)

(5) Begin by thinking about your own memories and writing them down. (6) Then interview your parents grandparents, and other relatives if possible. (7) You might consider asking some informal questions with a tape recorder running.
(8) Remember that it's often necessary for people to warm up to the task of talking about themselves and the past.

(C)

(9) When you've gotten as much information as you can by interviewing family members, do some more formal research. (10) Start at your local Library and ask where the genealogy section is. (11) It may also contain town or county archives, which hold documents such as birth certificates, death records, and other historical information. (12) From the library, proceed to a local courthouse, or the county clerk's office. (13) There you may find some of your family's marriage and divorce papers, voter records, and wills. (14) And don't forget the cemetery! (15) Headstones can help confirm dates, and family relationships too.

14. Sentence 1: **Researching and recording you're family history can be a fun and rewarding adventure.**

Which correction should be made to sentence 1?
(1) replace you're with your
(2) change history to History
(3) insert a comma after history
(4) insert a comma after fun
(5) no correction is necessary

15. Sentence 3: **What a gift to be past on to future generations!**

Which correction should be made to sentence 3?
(1) insert a comma after gift
(2) replace to be with too be
(3) replace past with passed
(4) insert a comma after on
(5) replace on to with on two

16. Sentence 6: **Then interview your parents grandparents, and other relatives if possible.**

Which is the best way to write the underlined portion of this sentence? If the original is the best way, choose option (1).
(1) parents grandparents, and other relatives
(2) parents grandparents and other relatives
(3) parents grandparents and other relatives,
(4) parents, grandparents, and other relatives
(5) parents grandparents, and other relatives,

17. Sentence 9: **When you've gotten as much information as you can by interviewing family members, do some more formal research.**

Which correction should be made to sentence 9?
(1) change you've to youv'e
(2) insert a comma after can
(3) replace by with buy
(4) remove the comma after members
(5) no correction is necessary

18. Sentence 10: **Start at your local Library and ask where the genealogy section is.**

Which correction should be made to sentence 10?
(1) change Library to library
(2) insert a comma after ask
(3) replace where with wear
(4) change genealogy to Genealogy
(5) no correction is necessary

19. Sentence 15: **Headstones can help confirm dates, and family relationships too.**

Which is the best way to write the underlined portion of this sentence? If the original is the best way, choose option (1).
(1) dates, and
(2) dates and
(3) dates. And
(4) dates, also
(5) dates

Part 2: Directions

In this part, you will read questions about paragraphs, not just sentences. Read each question carefully. Choose the one best answer from three possible choices. As you answer the questions, fill in numbers 20 through 25 on the grid on page 7. When you are finished, check your answers to Parts 1 and 2 on page 18. Use the chart on page 19 to help you plan your study as you watch the programs and work through this book.

Questions 20 through 22 refer to the following company memo.

To: All Company Employees

(A)

(1) Because security has become a major concern, we have devised a new security closing procedure. (2) The following procedure must be followed at the end of the day. (3) Failure to follow it will result in a written warning being placed in an employee's file. (4) Poor job performance and poor attendance are also grounds for firing an employee.

(B)

(5) At the close of the business day, the front and back doors must be locked with the new automated locking system. (6) This system requires one code for locking and another for opening. (7) The shift supervisor has both codes, so he or she will normally be responsible for this security step. (8) However, this procedure may not be possible at times. (9) An employee may need to work late. (10) In this case, the employee should get the locking code from the shift supervisor before he or she leaves. (11) The employee must also get permission to be in the building after hours.

(C)

(12) Security is important. (13) This company prides itself on its trustworthy and responsible employees. (14) In the past, you have helped keep the building secure and functioning. (15) If we continue to work together, we can keep our company a safe and productive place to work.

20. Read paragraph A again. Pay special attention to sentence 4: **Poor job performance and poor attendance are also grounds for firing an employee.**

    Which revision should be made to the placement of sentence 4?
    (1) Move sentence 4 to follow sentence 1.
    (2) Move sentence 4 to follow sentence 2.
    (3) Remove sentence 4.

21. Read paragraph B again. Which revision should be made to this paragraph?
    (1) The paragraph should be divided, and a new paragraph should begin with sentence 7.
    (2) The paragraph should be divided, and a new paragraph should begin with sentence 8.
    (3) The paragraph is fine as is.

22. Read paragraph C again. Pay special attention to sentence 12: **Security is important.**

    Which revision should be made to sentence 12?
    (1) Change sentence 12 to "The success of this security measure depends on each of you."
    (2) Change sentence 12 to "This company trusts its workers."
    (3) No revision is necessary.

Questions 23 through 25 refer to the following article.

The Danger of Gangs

(A)

(1) Many communities throughout the country have a problem with gangs. (2) There are different types of gangs, but every gang has a negative impact on a community.

(B)

(3) Neighborhood businesses suffer from gangs. (4) Customers avoid areas where gangs hang out. (5) A loss of customers means a loss of income for storeowners and other businesses.

(C)

(6) A business owner in a gang area must absorb the costs of thefts, high insurance, and the cleanup of graffiti. (7) Many of these costs are passed on to the customers that do come to the business.

(D)

(8) Neighborhood residents also suffer from gangs. (9) Obviously, the threat of violence from gangs brings fear to all. (10) Parents are especially concerned for their children's safety. (11) They may also fear that their children will become gang members themselves one day. (12) Everyone is afraid of getting hurt, whether on purpose or by accident.

(E)

(13) People can form neighborhood watch groups to look for gang activity. (14) They can work closely with the police and other agencies. (15) Most important, they can offer young people support, caring, and activities that are positive alternatives to gangs.

23. Read paragraphs B and C again. Which revision should be made to these paragraphs?
    (1) Paragraphs B and C should be joined.
    (2) Paragraph C should be removed.
    (3) The paragraphs are fine as is.

24. Read paragraph D again. Pay special attention to sentence 12: **Everyone is afraid of getting hurt, whether on purpose or by accident.**

    Which revision should be made to the placement of sentence 12?
    (1) Move sentence 12 to follow sentence 8.
    (2) Move sentence 12 to follow sentence 9.
    (3) Remove sentence 12.

25. Read paragraph E again. Which sentence would be most effective if inserted at the beginning of paragraph E?
    (1) Are you looking for a way to fight gangs?
    (2) Gangs are in many communities.
    (3) Business owners and residents can join together to fight gangs.

Answers and explanations are on page 18.

Part 3: Directions

Read the writing topic in the box. Use the steps outlined below it to write a paragraph about the topic. Then evaluate your work using the guidelines on page 19. In this way you will get a good idea of your strengths and challenges as a writer.

TOPIC

Fear is an emotion that every human being experiences.

Identify one thing you are afraid of, and explain why.

Planning

In the space below, write down everything you can think of when you read the topic above. Don't bother writing complete sentences, and don't worry about spelling. Your goal is to jot down as many ideas as you can. Spend **five minutes** on this step.

Ideas

Writing

Choose the ideas you want to include in your paragraph. Write a sentence that tells what the main point of your paragraph will be. Write this sentence at the top of the following page.

Now write the rest of your paragraph following that sentence. Use the ideas you chose from above. Spend **ten minutes** on this step.

Main point:

_____

_____

_____

_____

_____

_____

_____

_____

_____

_____

_____

_____

_____

_____

_____

_____

_____

_____

_____

_____

_____

_____

_____

_____

_____

_____

Improving

Read your paragraph and make any changes you think would improve your writing.
Neatly cross out or add ideas. Make corrections in grammar and spelling if necessary.
Spend **five minutes** on this step.

Evaluation guidelines are on page 19.

Pretest Answers and Explanations

1. **(5) together, we** A comma is needed after the thought *If we work together* at the beginning of the sentence.

2. **(4) insert and after the comma** Two complete thoughts cannot be joined with just a comma. A connecting word like *and* is also needed.

3. **(2) clerk. He** Two complete thoughts were run together in the original. The best way to correct this error is to make two complete sentences.

4. **(3) calendar because** The original sentence 8 is not actually a complete sentence. Answer choice (3) correctly attaches it to sentence 7.

5. **(1) spoke with the night manager and told her** This choice combines the meaning of the two short, choppy-sounding sentences into one smooth sentence: *I spoke with the night manager and told her we would not be staying that night.*

6. **(3) insert a comma after Wind** A comma is needed before the connecting word *and* in a sentence that joins two complete thoughts.

7. **(4) replace its with their** The singular pronoun *its* cannot refer to the plural noun *food manufacturers.* Using *their* corrects the error.

8. **(3) replace them with they** You need a subject pronoun *(they)* not an object pronoun *(them)* for the thought *they are the goals of food companies.*

9. **(2) are** The subject is plural *(marketing strategies)*, so the verb must be *are*, not *is.*

10. **(5) no correction is necessary** The sentence is correct as written.

11. **(3) changes pays to pay** The subject of the sentence is plural *(companies)*, so the verb *pay* is correct. Do not be confused by the interrupting phrase *in the food industry.*

12. **(2) have** The verb tense of this sentence is the present.

13. **(5) is** The correct verb form and tense for this sentence is *is. Been* is always an incomplete verb form.

14. **(1) replace you're with your** The contraction *you're* means *you are*, which is incorrect in this sentence. The correct homonym to use is the possessive pronoun *your.*

15. **(3) replace past with passed** The homonym *past* meaning "ago" is incorrect in this sentence; the past tense *passed* is correct.

16. **(4) parents, grandparents, and other relatives** Commas are needed to separate the items in a series of three or more: *parents, grandparents, and other relatives.*

17. **(5) no correction is necessary** The sentence is correct as written.

18. **(1) change Library to library** The common noun *library* does not name a specific place, so it should not be capitalized.

19. **(2) dates and** No comma is needed between two items: *dates and family relationships.*

20. **(3) remove sentence 4** A sentence about other reasons for firing an employee is not relevant to the paragraph. The paragraph is about the need to follow the new security procedure.

21. **(2) The paragraph should be divided, and a new paragraph should begin with sentence 8.** With sentence 8, the main idea shifts to what happens when an employee stays after the supervisor leaves. Therefore, this information should be a separate paragraph.

22. **(1) Change sentence 12 to "The success of this security measure depends on each of you."** The first sentence of the paragraph should tell the main point of the paragraph. This option does. The original sentence is too general.

23. **(1) Paragraphs B and C should be joined.** Both paragraphs B and C concern business owners and gangs, so the two should be combined.

24. **(2) Move sentence 12 to follow sentence 9.** This sentence is about everyone's concerns over getting hurt. It flows naturally from sentence 9, which talks about the fear of all. The next two sentences then talk about the fears of parents in particular.

25. **(3) Business owners and residents can join together to fight gangs.** This sentence ties the topics of the middle paragraphs (businesses and residents) with the ideas in the last paragraph (ways to fight gangs). It tells the main point of the last paragraph.

Pretest Evaluation

PARTS 1–2 DIRECTIONS: Check your answers on page 18. On the chart below, circle the numbers of the questions you got correct. In the last column, write the total number you got correct in each section. If you got more than 2 wrong in any section, pay particular attention to the programs and workbook pages listed.

Questions	Total Correct	Program
1, 2, 3, 4, 5, 6	___ / 6 correct	4: Effective Sentences Pages 80–99
7, 8, 9, 10, 11, 12, 13	___ / 7 correct	5: Grammar and Usage Pages 100–119
14, 15, 16, 17, 18, 19	___ / 6 correct	6: Spelling, Punctuation, and Capitalization Pages 120–139
20, 21, 22, 23, 24, 25	___ / 6 correct	3: Organized Writing Pages 60–79

PART 3 DIRECTIONS: Use the questions below to evaluate your writing sample. If possible, show your writing to a teacher, coworker, or fellow student for feedback.

Evaluation Guidelines

Planning

- How did you feel as you jotted down your ideas? Confident? Or anxious?
- Did you come up with enough ideas, or did you feel stuck and unable to think?
- Did most of the ideas you wrote down relate to the topic of fear?

Comments: _____

If you had trouble with this step of the writing process, pay particular attention to Program 2, workbook pages 42–45.

Writing

- Was it easy or difficult to put your ideas into complete sentences?
- Does your first sentence sum up all the ideas that follow in your paragraph?

Comments: _____

If you had trouble with this step of the writing process, pay particular attention to Program 2, workbook pages 46–49.

Improving

- Does your paragraph include all the ideas you want and need to tell a reader?
- Do you feel you found and corrected most of the mistakes in your paragraph?

Comments: _____

If you had trouble with this step of the writing process, pay particular attention to Program 2, workbook pages 50–53.

Getting Ideas on Paper

1. Think About the Topic

The program you are about to watch is about *Getting Ideas on Paper*. The point of this video is that writing is a way to express your ideas and feelings—to others or just for yourself.

In this program, you will see professional writers, writing teachers, and students. You will hear from teachers who urge you to start writing freely, without being afraid of making mistakes. One teacher will explain the difference between being the creator and being the editor. What do you think that means?

2. Prepare to Watch the Video

This program will give you lots of ideas about how to get your thoughts down on paper. One writer suggests that you list some things that make you who you are. Try it below:

My best qualities are _____

_____

People tell me that my worst qualities are _____

_____

You might have written something like: *My best qualities are my loyalty and willingness to work hard. People tell me that my worst qualities are my impatience and stubbornness.*

3. Preview the Questions

Read the questions under *Think About the Program* on the next page and keep them in mind as you watch the program. After you watch, use the questions to review the main ideas in the program.

LESSON GOALS

WRITING SKILLS

- Use writing to express your ideas and feelings
- Write personal letters and e-mail
- Write a personal story

WRITER'S TOOL

- Keep a journal

GED ESSAY CONNECTION

- Draw on your personal experience

GED REVIEW

EXTRA PRACTICE, PP. 140–143

- Free Writing
- Letters and E-Mail
- Personal Stories
- GED Essay

4. Study the Vocabulary

Review the terms to the right. Understanding the meaning of writing vocabulary will help you understand the video and the rest of the lesson.

WATCH THE PROGRAM

As you watch the program, pay special attention to the host who introduces or summarizes major ideas that you need to learn about. The host will also tell you important information about the GED Writing Test.

AFTER YOU WATCH

1. Think About the Program

What are some activities you can try in order to help you start writing?

What are some of the different reasons people have for keeping journals?

What are some personal activities that can help you practice your writing?

2. Make the Connection

Several people in this program talk about writing *your* story. What is a time, an event, or an idea that is an important part of who you are? What are the stories behind it?

TERMS

body—the part of a letter that contains the message

closing—a word or phrase that ends a letter

details—examples, reasons, and specific bits of information that help writing come alive

e-mail—electronic mail; mail sent from one computer to another

fields—areas on a computer screen on which to enter information

format—the way a written message is presented

free writing—writing whatever comes into your head for a set period of time; a technique for getting ideas to write about

journal—a daily record in which a person writes down his or her thoughts and experiences

return address—the address of the writer, written at the top of a letter

sequence—the order in which events happened

zooming—a way to get ideas and details by focusing on yourself; on family, relatives, and friends; and on society

WRITING SKILLS

"The first step in any writing assignment is recognizing that you have something to say and that writing is a good way to say it."

Expressing Yourself

Getting Started

When you start to write, you are faced with a blank piece of paper or a blank computer screen. It can be hard to get started. As you saw in the program, even experienced writers sometimes need help.

To help themselves get started, professional writers have developed some good techniques. Adult students can use the same techniques that professional writers use. You will learn some of these techniques in this lesson and throughout this book.

Two techniques are especially good to get started with writing:
- free writing
- keeping a journal

Free Writing

Free writing means writing whatever comes into your head. You put your pen to paper, start writing, and keep writing. The only rules are these: Don't stop until a set period of time is over. Don't worry about your spelling or punctuation. Don't stop to correct what you've written. Don't even try to write in complete sentences. Just keep writing.

When the time is up, stop and read what you have written. You will find some useful and interesting ideas. You will find *your* ideas—thoughts you may not even have known you had.

Free writing is a helpful technique when you can't think of ideas to write about. It is also useful when you feel "stuck"—when you have a few ideas but need more.

Here are the steps for free writing:
1. If you have a topic to write about, put that topic at the top of your paper.
2. Set a timer for five or ten minutes.
3. Start to write. Don't lift your pen from the paper.
4. Stop only when you hear the timer go off.

On the next page is an example of free writing about the topic of true friendship.

What is a true friend?

True friendship true friendship. What does true friendship mean to me?
Dwayne. Dwayne is a true friend of mine. He's always been there when I
need him. I can trust him. And he knows he can trust me. Like the time I
told him how I felt about Shana. He kept my secret. He didn't tell. A lot
of guys would have. He's also done a lot for me. Helped me out. Like when
I was moving. He took off work and drove the rental truck. Course he
knows I'd do the same for him. I helped him when his car was broke. We
can depend on each other to help. What else makes him a true friend? He's
honest. Yeah, he tells me things like when I'm getting a little too loud and
wild but he wouldn't say anything to hurt my feelings. Or anyone else for
that matter. Dwayne's just a great guy.

GETTING IDEAS ON PAPER ▪ PRACTICE 1

Practice free writing now. Get some ideas to answer this question: *What does success mean to you?* Set a timer for five minutes. Start on the lines below. Write whatever comes into your head. Continue on another sheet of paper if you need to. After five minutes are up, stop.

What does success mean to me?

_____

_____

_____

_____

_____

_____

_____

_____

_____

_____

_____

_____

Feedback starts on page 178.
For more practice with free writing, see page 140.

WRITING SKILLS

Journals

Think back to the video program *Getting Ideas on Paper*. In the video, several writers talked about their notebooks and journals. A **journal** is a daily record in which a person writes down his or her thoughts and experiences.

People write in journals for many reasons:
- to record what happens in their lives
- to help them think about problems and issues
- to get ideas for more writing

Have you ever kept a journal, or have you ever wanted to? Can you think of some good reasons for you to keep a journal? Write them here.

_____

_____

_____

_____

Here's an example of a journal entry. In it, the writer is "thinking on paper" about a problem.

> I just don't know what to do about Dad. He seems so lonely now that he's all alone. He just sits and watches TV—a lot of TV—too much TV. He needs to be more active, for his health. He needs to get outdoors more. Breathe some fresh air. He really needs some companionship too. When he comes over for dinner, it's hard to get him to talk about much. He really loves to pet our dog, Jake, though. Sometimes I think Jake's the only reason Dad agrees to visit! Maybe having his own dog would help him. A dog could be a good companion for him. They could go for walks together. I think I'll take Dad to the animal shelter this weekend. See if he takes a liking to one.

This writer jotted down some of her thoughts about a problem with her father. In the middle of writing, she realized what she might do to help solve it. Sometimes, just writing about a problem can help you make a change or a decision.

Do you have a problem—or maybe two—that you could write about in a journal? Make a list of problems or issues on your mind right now:

_____

_____

_____

_____

_____

_____

Did something special or unusual happen to you today? A journal is also a good place to note special experiences. You can jot down a memory that you don't want to forget. For example, here's what one writer wrote in his journal one evening:

> Darius took his first step this afternoon! He was sitting on the floor at Mom's, and I went to pick him up. When he saw me. He squealed and grinned. Then he stood up and took a step toward me! He fell right back down on his big Diaper. But that was his first step, and I saw it myself. Mom and I were so excited.

The writer above made some mistakes. (Can you find them? Look below.*) That's OK. In a journal entry, you don't have to worry about being "correct." Don't worry about your spelling, grammar, or capitalization. Just let go, and write whatever comes to you.

As you work through this series, you may want to keep a journal about your accomplishments and challenges. On page 34, you will get some ideas about how to start your own journal.

GETTING IDEAS ON PAPER ▪ PRACTICE 2

For now, write a journal entry. Here are some suggestions to get you started. Choose one, and fill up the page!

- Write about an event that happened recently.
- Write about a problem that's on your mind.
- Write about something you saw or heard that made you think.

_____

_____

_____

_____

_____

_____

_____

_____

_____

_____

_____

_____

Feedback starts on page 178.

*The mistakes are the incomplete sentence, or fragment, *When he saw me.* and the capital *D* in *Diaper.*

"Everybody has a writer within them who needs to be freed!"

Writing Letters and E-mail

Writing is a good way to keep in touch with friends and relatives. Writing to someone you know can be easy and pleasant. If you have a computer, you might send **e-mail**. (The *e* is short for "electronic.") Otherwise, you might choose to send a personal letter.

What's the Difference?

The speed of e-mail is amazing. An e-mail message can be sent from one computer to another in seconds. In contrast, regular mail seems as slow as a snail! Speed is the biggest difference between e-mail and post-office "snail mail."

But there are other differences between an e-mail message and a letter sent by mail. E-mail has to be written on a computer. A letter may be written on a computer and printed, or it may be written by hand. Handwritten letters are more personal than typed letters.

Another difference is **format**, or the way the message is presented. Both the e-mail message and the personal letter have their own special ways to show basic information:

- the date
- the writer's name
- the name of the person being written to

E-mail and letters do have one thing in common. Most people love to receive them!

Thinking of the Reader

The best way to get e-mail and letters is to write e-mail and letters. The people you write to may not all write back—but some of them will. Plus, you'll be practicing your writing. You'll also make friends and relatives feel glad to hear from you.

What should you write about? Ask yourself what your reader would want to know. People like to know about your life! Here are some possible topics:

- **Work**—a new job, a different boss, or a skill you just learned
- **Family**—babies, birthdays, or just what everyday family life is like
- **Projects and hobbies**—anything from crafts to car repair
- **Sports**—a team you play on or coach, a team you just love to watch
- **Movies and music**—a great film you've seen, a cool new CD you've heard

1. Think of some people you could write letters or e-mail messages to. On the lines below, write their names. Then list three topics that would interest each reader.

   Example: my Aunt Gloria

   Topics:
   Gloria loves hearing about my daughter

   I'm having a hard time with my diet but lost five pounds so far

   ask her how my cousin Lupe is doing with her new baby

   Reader 1: _____

   Topics:

   _____

   _____

   _____

   Reader 2: _____

   Topics:

   _____

   _____

   _____

2. Now pick one reader and one topic. Pretend you are writing that person a letter. Write at least three sentences about the topic here:

   Dear _____,

   _____

   _____

   _____

   _____

   _____

   _____

3. On a separate sheet of paper, continue your personal letter. Write at least three sentences about each of the other two topics you listed for that person.

Feedback and writing model start on page 178.

WRITING SKILLS

Formats of Letters and E-mail

Personal letters follow guidelines about what to write and where to write it. Read each guideline that follows. Then look for that element on the sample personal letter below.

- Write your own address (the **return address**) at the top of the page.
- Underneath, put the date—month, day, and year.
- Begin with *Dear* and the person's name, followed by a comma.
- The **body** of the letter is your message. It can have one or more paragraphs. Indent each paragraph.
- End with a **closing**, a word or phrase such as *Your friend, Love,* or *Sincerely,* followed by a comma.
- Under the closing, sign your name by hand, even if the letter is typed.

The format of an e-mail message is set up for you. At the top are **fields**, or areas to write in, headed by *From, To,* and *Subject*. Next to *To*, you insert the e-mail address of the person you are writing to. Next to *Subject*, you insert your topic. You don't have to insert your name or the date because the computer does that for you. When the e-mail message appears on your reader's computer, this information appears automatically.

Some people write very informally in e-mail messages, as you can see below.

Personal Letter	Received E-mail Message
645 E. Wakeberry Rd. Chapelton, NC 23654 May 12, 2003 Dear Aunt Gloria, 　I'm trying to write more these days. I know you like to hear about Ava. She is in second grade, and she can read chapter books by herself now. Sometimes she reads to herself at bedtime. It's a big change. 　My diet is really hard, but I'm not giving up. I've lost five pounds, and I hear the first five are the hardest to lose. 　Hope you are fine. Write back and tell me all about Lupe's new baby! Love, *Rosa*	**From:** marc@sev-us.com (John Marc) **To:** kimmie@yoohoo.com **Sent:** Monday, May 12, 2003, 5:05 PM **Subject:** vacation plans! We'll be on our way to the beach by this time next week! Do you have directions to the motel? It's called Beach Town, and it's on the right side of the highway, east of Carol Beach. You've seen it before, right? We'll bring some groceries with us. Last year you had some great beach gear. Can you bring all that stuff again? Mom says you're dating somebody. Want to bring your new friend too? See ya soon!

1. In Practice 3, you actually wrote the body of a personal letter. Copy the body onto the letter format below. Add the other elements of a personal letter.

> **Write your return address here.** ➝ _____
> _____

> **Write the date here.** ➝ _____

Dear _____,

_____

_____

_____

_____

_____

_____

_____

_____

> **Write the closing here.** ➝ _____

> **Sign your name here.** ➝ _____

2. On another sheet of paper, write a letter to your other reader from Practice 3, on page 27. Use the topics you already listed, or think of some new ones. Follow the guidelines and format shown on page 28.

3. Suppose you want to invite a friend to go to a movie with you. Write an e-mail message in the format below. The friend's e-mail address has already been filled in.

> To: msmith@mindlink.com

> Subject:

>
>
>
>
>

Checklist and writing model start on page 178.

For more practice with letters and e-mail, see page 141.

"There's nobody in the world who doesn't have a story to tell."

Writing a Personal Story

Your Own Story

Writing a story about an event in your life can be an interesting process. Very often, writers discover something new about the events they write about. They may even discover something new about themselves. This might happen to you! Let's find out. In the next few pages, you'll work on writing a personal story.

A good way to begin is to think of a few past events that were important to you. These events might be—

- **"turning points"**—moments that really changed your life
- **times** that were particularly happy or sad
- **events** that just stick in your mind, even if you're not sure why

Write down some events from your life that you might want to write about:

_____

_____

_____

Bring Your Story to Life

What makes a story come to life? A good story helps the reader picture what's going on. You can "draw" this picture for your reader by including specific information about—

- **Time and place:** What time of day and year was it? Where did the event happen, and what was it like there?
- **People**: Who was there? What kinds of people were they? Why were they there?
- **Action:** What was the "big moment" that really sticks out in your memory? What events led up to it? What events followed it?

Anna is writing a story about her first day at work. She started by making notes about the time and place, people, and action. She numbered the events in **sequence**—the order in which they happened. To help her remember, she **visualized**. That means she pictured in her own mind what happened.

Time and place: cold winter morning, small hotel restaurant on a busy highway, booths and tables, big plastic menus, pink & green decor

People: Ernesto (manager), Judith (waitress), Tina (hostess). Didn't know any of them. Ernesto had to train me and run restaurant at same time

Action:

The big moment: handling a table of six guys and getting no tip

Events before and after:

1. started at 5:30 in the morning
2. Ernesto let me in back door, introduced me
3. I put on apron, got order pad, began my training
4. Ernesto unlocked front door at 6:00
5. he helped me at first, then I was on my own
6. six loud guys walked in, pushed two tables together in my section
7. hard time taking their order, things got mixed up
8. they left without tipping me
9. Judith told me to never mind, I'd do better
10. got back to work, but learned something

GETTING IDEAS ON PAPER ■ PRACTICE 5

Now it's your turn to start writing a story. Pick one of the events you listed on page 30. Answer these questions with information you could include in the story. You don't need to write complete sentences.

1. **Time and place:** Where did the event happen, and what was it like there? What time of day and year was it?

   _____

   _____

2. **People:** Who was there? What kinds of people were they? Why were they there?

   _____

   _____

3. **Action:** What was the "big moment" that really sticks out in your memory? What events led up to it and followed it? (Number them in sequence below.)

   The big moment: _____

   Events before and after: _____

   _____

   _____

   _____

   _____

   Feedback starts on page 178.

Why Does Your Story Matter?

Anna's first day as a waitress meant something important to her. After all, she chose that event to write about.

Anna jotted down a few notes about why her story mattered to her:

> Looking back, I realize how much I learned about people and work. Always liked meeting people. Thought I'd like waiting tables. Learned that people didn't come to restaurant to meet me! They want good food and good service.

You probably feel the same way about the story you've started. You chose an event to write about because it matters to you. If you tell your reader why your story is important to you, the reader will care more about it.

Take a few minutes now to write your thoughts about why *your* story matters:

Looking back, _____

_____

_____

_____

_____

_____

The Whole Story

Your reader will understand your story better if it has a beginning, a middle, and an end. Here's a way to do that using the notes you've already made:

- **Beginning:** Set the stage.
  Describe the time and place. Introduce the people.
- **Middle:** Describe the action.
  Show what happened in sequence. Emphasize the "big moment."
- **End:** Look back.
  Tell your reader why your story is important.

You can write a paragraph for each of these parts of the story. The paragraphs don't all have to be the same length. Sometimes the beginning and ending paragraphs are short.

If your story is really long, you might need more than one paragraph in the middle.

On the next page, you'll find Anna's story about her first day on the job. As you read it, notice that her story has a beginning, a middle, and an end.

Breakfast Rush at the Super-Stop Cafe

Set the stage. → I started my first waitress job at 5:30 in the morning on a cold February day. Ernesto, the manager at the Super-Stop Cafe, let me in the back door. He introduced me to the cook, the hostess, and the other waitress. I put on my apron and got my order pad. Ernesto began my training session, and at 6:00 he unlocked the front door.

Describe the action. → Things happened fast. I had eight tables and part of the counter to wait on. Ernesto helped me with my first few orders. But by 7:00, I was on my own, and the morning rush was on. Everybody was hungry and in a hurry. I'll never forget one group of six guys. They ignored Tina, the hostess, grabbed menus, and pushed two tables together in the back, right in my section. When I took their order, they all talked at once, teasing each other and giving me a hard time about getting their specials right. I got mixed up, but I was scared to ask them to repeat their orders. Big mistake! When I brought their food, it seemed like everything was wrong—eggs cooked wrong, omelets filled wrong, hash browns not brown enough. They didn't have time to send the food back, so they just growled at me. They were my biggest table of the morning, and they left NO TIP. I nearly cried. Judith came over, put her arm around me, and told me not to worry, that I'd do better with my next big table. I went back to work, promising myself she was right.

Look back. → I learned a lot that day. I thought being a waitress would be easy because I liked to meet people and talk, and people always liked me. I didn't understand that waiting tables is about getting it right and getting it fast. But guess what? Here's the funny thing. If you get it right and you get it fast, then the folks <u>will</u> like you. Those six guys got to be my regulars, and after a while, we kidded around like we were old friends.

GETTING IDEAS ON PAPER ■ PRACTICE 6

On a separate sheet of paper, write your personal story. Use your notes on pages 31 and 32. The *Time and place* and *People* notes on page 31 will become the beginning of your story. The *Action* notes will become the middle. The *Looking back* notes on page 32 will become the end.

Add information and interesting details as you write. Try to use complete sentences. For now, however, don't worry about correct spelling and grammar.

Checklist starts on page 178.
For more practice with personal stories, see page 142.

Keeping a Journal

In the video program, writer Frank Walker talked about using a journal to "capture" what's going on around him in his life. You have already worked with journal entries on pages 24 and 25.

A journal is one way to help you think about your life at present. A journal also allows you to look back on the past. You can reread your journal later on—even years later. A journal helps you think about where you came from as well as where you're going.

Right now, you're on a journey toward the GED Writing Test. Keep a journal along the way. Someday, you'll be able to see how far you've come!

Your journal is for—

- recording events in your life
- writing practice
- sorting out problems, thoughts, and ideas
- anything else you want to put in

There are no right or wrong topics in a journal. Also, you don't have to worry about whether your writing is correct.

A **journal** is a personal notebook. In a journal, you can write about events in your life and whatever else is important to you.

Instructions for Starting a Journal

1. **Get a notebook.** Size is important. What kind of handwriting do you have? If you write large, make sure the notebook lines are wide enough to write comfortably. Does a big blank page look like too much space to you? Then buy a small notebook. Do you want to carry your journal in your pocket? Then get a notepad—or two!

2. **Write your name in front of the journal.** If you are in a class, ask your teacher if there are any guidelines that you should follow. If so, write them in front also.

   An important note: Some teachers like to read their students' journals and write back. If you're writing in a journal that your teacher will read, you may want to keep some things private.

3. **Decide where and when you will write.** Where would you like to write in your journal—at home? at the library? at work on your lunch break?

   Can you think of any tricks that might encourage you to write? For example, maybe you will promise yourself to write half a page for every half hour of TV you watch.

One student began his journal this way:

> I don't know if I can ever learn to write well. But I'll never find out unless I try. I'm going to write in this journal every day. Well, I might not make it every day. But the guy in the video said to write at least a few times a week. I can do that. I'm going to carry my journal on the subway with me on the way to work. Every time I get a seat, I'll write a paragraph. If I can do that, I should write something pretty often. I don't really know what I should write about. Maybe I'll start by writing down what I notice while I'm riding the subway. There sure are a lot of interesting faces on the train.

Write your ideas for where and when you will write in your journal below. Include any encouraging tricks you might use.

_____

_____

_____

Give Yourself Time

If you are not used to writing, set a certain amount of time for writing in your journal. You could start with ten minutes. Don't worry about how *much* you write in ten minutes—just congratulate yourself for writing for ten minutes! If you write for ten minutes almost every day, you will write about an hour every week! Short sessions add up.

USING THE WRITER'S TOOL ▪ KEEP A JOURNAL

1. Buy a notebook to use for your journal.

2. Write your name inside the front cover.

3. Write today's date, and begin!

    Write about what happened to you today. Or if you like, copy one of these starters into your journal and write for ten minutes:

    This week, I'm going to try…
    I love _____ because …
    Something I've always wanted to figure out is …
    If I could change one thing in my life, it would be …
    Right now, my most important responsibilities in life are …
    The most beautiful or inspiring scene I've seen lately was …
    My greatest strength is …

    Feedback starts on page 178.

Drawing on Your Personal Experience

In this lesson you have practiced free writing and writing a journal entry. You have also written a letter, an e-mail message, and a personal story. These are all important writing tasks in and of themselves. Even better, they prepare you for writing an essay on the GED Writing Test.

On the GED Test, you will have 45 minutes to write an essay. (You will learn more about the essay and how it is scored as you work through this book.) One of the best ways to write a high-scoring essay is to include many relevant details. If you look at the GED Essay Scoring Guide on page 192, you will see that one of the five scoring categories is "Development and Details."

What are details? **Details** are the bits and pieces of information that make your writing come alive. They are—

- **examples** that help show exactly what you mean
- **reasons** that help support and explain your ideas
- **specific information** that helps your reader picture what you are writing about

Where do details come from? They come from you:

- what you have seen in your lifetime
- what you have learned, not only in school but also in living day to day
- what you have experienced in life

Details are important in all good writing. When you wrote the e-mail, letter, and personal story for this lesson, you used details you had gathered from your life. Details are so important in a GED essay that the directions for the essay often *tell* you to use your **personal observations, knowledge, and experiences** when you write.

Here is the kind of essay topic you might find on the GED Writing Test.

TOPIC

Stress is a part of most people's lives.

In your essay, explain the various ways people deal with stress. Use your personal observations, knowledge, and experiences to support your essay.

On the next page are two sample paragraphs written on that topic. The first paragraph answers the question, but it is very general. The second paragraph is developed with lots of details. As you read the two paragraphs, think about how the writer used personal experience to add details.

VERY GENERAL—NO DETAILS:

> Stress is a part of most people's lives. People deal with stress in various ways. Some people, for example, try to relax to forget their stress.

DEVELOPED WITH DETAILS:

> Stress is a part of most people's lives. Yet how people deal with their stress varies greatly. Some people, for example, seek relaxation. They may turn down the lights and listen to soothing music—classical or quiet jazz. A warm bath in candlelight can ease stress too. When I'm feeling stressed, I spread out my mat, take a few deep breaths, and meditate.

Both writers start out basically the same way—that some people reduce stress by relaxing. But the second paragraph doesn't stop there. It includes *examples* of relaxing activities: turned-down lights, soothing music, warm bath, and candlelight. It even gives the writer's *personal experience* with relaxation.

All these details help you understand what the writer means by relaxing to reduce stress. They make the paragraph strong and effective. Details are essential for a good score on the GED Essay.

GED ESSAY PRACTICE

DRAW ON EXPERIENCE FOR DEVELOPMENT AND DETAILS

1. Here is another general statement that relates to the essay topic on stress: "Other people prefer physical activities to release their stress."

    Ask yourself: *What physical activity have I seen people do to release stress? What have I read or heard about? What do I do to release stress?*

    Write some details below.

    _____

    _____

2. Here is a third general statement that relates to the essay topic on stress: "Some people, however, don't deal with their stress, or they release it in unhealthy ways."

    Ask yourself: *How have I seen people deal with stress in unhealthy ways? What have I read or heard about? Do I (or does someone I know) have a problem with stress?*

    Write some details below.

    _____

    _____

Writing models start on page 178.
For more practice with development and details, see page 143.

GED Writing Review

Read this example of an essay topic you might find on the GED Writing Test.

> **TOPIC**
>
> How much value do people place on honesty these days?
>
> In your essay, explain whether you think people are generally honest or dishonest. Use your personal observations, knowledge, and experiences.

A. Look for development and details.

Here is a paragraph written about the topic above. Read it carefully. Does the writer support the ideas with details?

> People say that honesty is the best policy. However, many people don't really follow that belief. In fact, sometimes honesty is not always the best policy. In general, though, I think we could all be more honest with each other. That would make for a better society.

1. *"However, many people don't really follow that belief."* Is this general statement supported by details? Write at least one specific detail to support it.

    _____

    _____

2. *"Sometimes honesty is not always the best policy."* Is this general statement supported by details? Write at least one specific detail to support it.

    _____

    _____

3. *"We could all be more honest with each other. That would make for a better society."* Is this general statement supported by details? Write at least one specific detail to support it.

    _____

    _____

B. Develop your own details.

Writers have developed several good techniques for thinking of details. One way is free writing. Another way is **zooming**. Have you ever focused a camera to take a picture? You zoom in to take a close-up. You zoom out to get a broad, panoramic picture. Each kind of shot gives you a different view and shows you different details.

Likewise, you can zoom your mind to focus on a topic from different views to get different details. First, you zoom in on yourself for a close-up. Then you zoom back a bit to look at your friends, family, and relatives. Finally, you zoom out to look at society, including people in general as well as TV, radio, magazines, and newspapers.

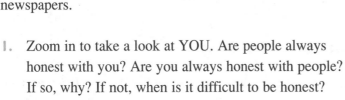

1. Zoom in to take a look at YOU. Are people always honest with you? Are you always honest with people? If so, why? If not, when is it difficult to be honest?

   _____

   _____

2. Zoom back to take a look at FAMILY, FRIENDS, and RELATIVES. Are other people always honest with them? Are they always honest with other people? Have they told you stories or experiences they have had with honesty or dishonesty?

   _____

   _____

3. Zoom out to take a look at SOCIETY. Are people in general honest? What have you seen in real life? What examples have you seen or heard about on TV or the radio? What have you read about in magazines or newspapers?

   _____

   _____

4. On another sheet of paper, write the following:

   a. two sentences with details about honesty concerning you

   b. two sentences with details about honesty concerning your family, friends, or relatives

   c. two sentences with details about honesty concerning society

C. Write a letter.

Think of the most exciting thing or the funniest thing that happened to you this past year. On another sheet of paper, write a letter to a friend telling about it. Be sure to include enough details. Answering these questions can help you:

- Pretend you were someone else watching the exciting or funny event happen. What exactly would that person see and hear?
- How did you feel? Did your emotions change from beginning to end?

Writing models and checklists start on page 178.

The Writing Process

LESSON GOALS

WRITING SKILLS

- Use different techniques to come up with ideas
- Organize your ideas and write a first draft
- Revise and edit your own writing

WRITER'S TOOL

- Make a portfolio

GED ESSAY CONNECTION

- Respond to the topic

GED REVIEW

EXTRA PRACTICE, PP. 144–147

- Brainstorm and Cluster
- Outline
- Revise and Edit
- GED Essay

1. Think About the Topic

You are about to watch a program on *The Writing Process*. This video shows you how to take an idea and turn it into a finished piece of writing using a step-by-step system.

In this program, teachers, students, and writers discuss the different steps in the writing process. You will hear museum exhibit designers talk about how they use a similar process to solve the problems they face on the job. Think of a time you have faced a problem. What steps did you take to solve it?

2. Prepare to Watch the Video

You will hear people in this video discuss brainstorming as a way to come up with ideas. In brainstorming, you write down anything you can think of that is related to a topic. Try to briefly brainstorm five or six ideas on the following subject:

The time I was most frightened: _____

_____

_____

_____

_____

_____

Here is an example of what a brief brainstorm list might look like: *plane ride, alone, first time, raining, lightning.*

3. Preview the Questions

Read the questions under *Think About the Program* on the next page and keep them in mind as you watch the program. After you watch, use the questions to review the main ideas in the program.

4. Study the Vocabulary

Review the terms to the right. Understanding the meaning of writing vocabulary will help you understand the video and the rest of the lesson.

WATCH THE PROGRAM

As you watch the program, pay special attention to the host who introduces or summarizes major ideas that you need to learn about. The host will also tell you important information about the GED Writing Test.

AFTER YOU WATCH

1. Think About the Program

What stages are involved in creating a piece of writing?

What are some ways of coming up with and organizing ideas?

Why is it important to write a rough draft before you revise or edit your work?

Will you think of the writing process as a strict rule or a helpful guideline to follow?

2. Make the Connection

Throughout this video, we see a class working on their responses to the sample topic "Who is your hero and why?" How would you respond to this topic?

brainstorming—writing down all ideas that come to mind

clustering—making a pattern of ideas around a main topic

cut and paste—to take words from one place in a computer document and move them to another

edit—to correct word choice, spelling, punctuation, and capitalization

first draft—the first version of a piece of writing

portfolio—an organized collection of a writer's work

purpose—the reason for writing

revise—to improve the content or organization of a piece of writing

supporting ideas—ideas that support the thesis of a piece of writing by explaining and illustrating it

thesis—the main point that a writer wants to make in a piece of writing

"You need to be in a flexible state—that's when you're going to come across that new idea that you never thought of before."

Coming Up with Ideas

Why Are You Writing?

As you learned in the video, writing is a process. It is a process that people use for different reasons. Below are some common reasons, or **purposes**, for writing and some types of writing for each purpose. Underline the purposes for writing you have had in the past. Then underline the types of writing you have done to meet those purposes.

Purposes for Writing	Types of Writing
To show what you know at school	Answers to questions, paragraph or essay for assignment or test, report
To explain or inform at work	Memo, note, letter, comments on form, report
To express an opinion	Letter to the editor, complaint letter
To connect with friends and family	Personal letter, e-mail, thank-you note, invitation
To be creative, to think about your life	Journal, story, poem, personal essay

Why you are writing helps you figure out *what* to write. Keep your purpose in mind. Then you will have an easier time with the first step in the writing process—coming up with ideas.

Brainstorming

Remember the museum exhibit designers in the video? They described one way to come up with ideas—**brainstorming**. They never shut out any ideas, no matter how crazy, in this very creative stage of their work.

Suppose you are faced with a writing assignment and don't know what to write. You can tap into the power of brainstorming. Here's how:

1. Set a certain amount of time.
2. During that time, write down any ideas you have.
3. Don't worry that an idea is too extreme or silly. Don't even take time to judge your ideas. (You will not use all the ideas you come up with.) Let your mind work freely.

Marc is practicing essay writing in his adult education class. He got this writing topic from his teacher: *What's your most important goal in life right now, and how could you work to achieve it?*

Here is the list of ideas Marc brainstormed:

How I can buy a home

research mortgage options

apply for first-time home buyers' program

look at different neighborhoods

we care about school district

teach the kids importance of owning a home

want a big yard

could sell the car to reduce monthly expenses

join warehouse club for groceries

save money on vacations by staying with family or doing things at home

don't eat out, even fast food is expensive for a family

fast food isn't good for you anyway

we're going to treat ourselves for Sophie's 8th grade graduation

no paid baby-sitters or full-price movies

THE WRITING PROCESS ▪ PRACTICE I

Now try to brainstorm. Suppose you want to write a personal piece. Your reader will be your teacher or a close friend. Your purpose in writing will be to share an important goal and your plans to meet it.

Write down a goal you would like to achieve within the next year or two. Then brainstorm a list of ideas about how you could achieve this goal.

My goal is _____

How I could achieve this goal: _____

_____

_____

_____

_____

_____

_____

_____

Feedback starts on page 179.

For more practice with brainstorming, see page 144.

Clustering

On the video program, you saw a teacher show the technique of **clustering** on a blackboard. A cluster is a pattern of ideas. In the center of the cluster is the main topic. Ideas are written around the topic. Circles and lines show how the ideas are related.

Many writers find that clustering helps them to think creatively. Maybe you will too!

Dorothy has been writing stories about her life to share with her children and grandchildren. These younger generations never met her father, who died when he was 40. Dorothy used clustering to help her remember details for a story about her father:

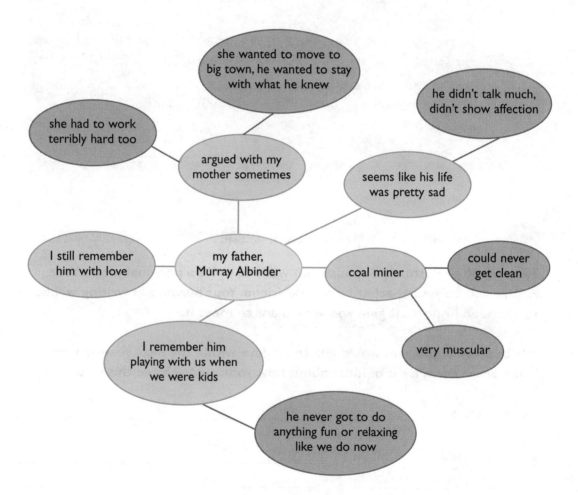

Look at the groups of details that surround the main topic. As Dorothy thought of new ideas, she added them. Then she drew lines to connect them to related ideas.

A cluster does not have to have a certain shape. There are many ways to connect the different ideas and details that come to you. Like brainstorming, there's no right answer, just lots of possibilities.

Here are the steps for clustering:

1. Get a blank, unlined sheet of paper.
2. Write your topic in a few words in the center. Draw a circle around it.
3. Write ideas about the topic around it. Connect them with lines to the main topic.
4. Write details around the ideas. Connect them any way that makes sense.
5. Don't judge your thoughts as you're making the cluster—just write down whatever comes to you.

THE WRITING PROCESS ▪ PRACTICE 2

Suppose you, like Dorothy, want to write a story about an important person in your life. Choose a person to write about. Then follow the steps above to make a cluster. You can begin with the beginning of a cluster below and add to it, or you can start on a fresh sheet of paper.

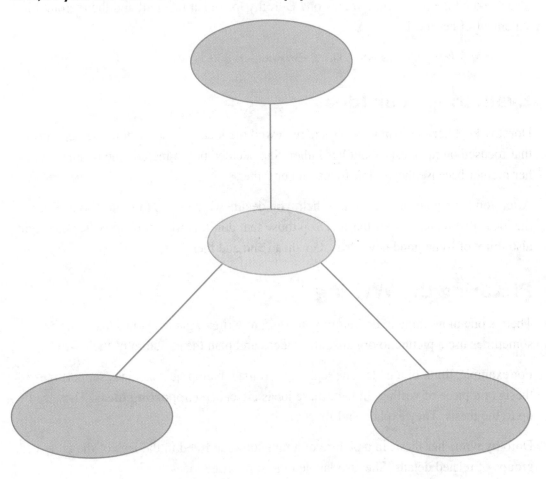

Feedback starts on page 179.
For more practice with clustering, see page 144.

> *"Look for the different points that fit together." Then, "Let yourself go. Let the words tumble through your pencil. . . . You can do some amazing things."*

Organizing and Writing a First Draft

What's Your Point?

Now that you have practiced brainstorming and clustering, you have ideas to write about. There are three more things to do, however, before you can begin writing.

First, figure out the point you want to make. When you write, you get to give your opinion, share an insight, or explain an idea. In fact, everything you write should focus on that opinion, insight, or idea. In writing, this focal point is called by different names. On the video program, it is called a thesis.

The **thesis** of a piece of writing is the *main* point the writer wants to make.

Review Dorothy's cluster of ideas about her father on page 44. What point do all the ideas, taken together, seem to focus on? Dorothy looked at them all and then wrote this statement of her thesis:

My father's life was hard, but I remember him with love.

Evaluating Your Ideas

Dorothy kept her thesis in mind as she reviewed the ideas in her cluster. She kept those that focused on the thesis about her father. She decided not to include the details about her mother because they didn't focus on her father.

After you have your thesis, use it to help you decide which ideas to write about. Keep the ideas that relate to your thesis. Drop those that don't. During this process, you might also think of some good new ideas. Go ahead and add them!

Picturing the Writing

There's one more thing to do before you begin to write: organize your ideas. Writers sometimes use a picture to organize their ideas and plan the structure of their writing.

For example, think of a table. The legs support the tabletop, just as ideas support the thesis of a piece of writing. In fact, these ideas are called **supporting ideas**. They lead up to the thesis. They explain and illustrate it.

Dorothy wrote her thesis in a picture of a tabletop. She filled in the legs of the table with groups of related details. She also labeled the supporting ideas.

Here is how Dorothy pictured her ideas.

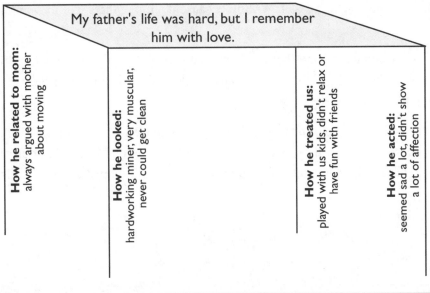

My father's life was hard, but I remember him with love.

How he related to mom: always argued with mother about moving

How he looked: hardworking miner, very muscular, never could get clean

How he treated us: played with us kids, didn't relax or have fun with friends

How he acted: seemed sad a lot, didn't show a lot of affection

THE WRITING PROCESS ▪ PRACTICE 3

Review the cluster you created for Practice 2, page 45. Then complete the steps below.

1. Write a thesis statement for a piece of writing based on your cluster. Remember, the thesis is the main point you want to make about your topic—in this case, the main point about the person.

   Thesis statement: _____

   _____

2. Evaluate the ideas in your cluster. Cross out ideas that don't relate to the thesis. Add ideas if they seem to fit.

3. See what groups of related ideas you can form. Give each group a label.

4. In the space below, draw a picture to organize your ideas. You might use a four-legged table or a three-legged stool. You could also use five pillars holding up a ceiling. Your picture will depend on the number of groups of ideas in your cluster.

Feedback starts on page 179.

Outlining

Some writers enjoy picturing their writing because it's fun. Others like the simplicity of outlining.

Maybe you have made outlines before. Some outlines look complicated, with different numerals and letters. But all an outline really needs to show is how your thesis, supporting ideas, and details fit together.

Marc organized his brainstormed list about buying a house with an outline. Like Dorothy, he started with a thesis statement. Also like Dorothy, Marc did not use every detail from his list. He came up with supporting ideas and grouped related details under them:

> Thesis: My whole family can work together to buy a home.
>
> Supporting Idea 1: Learn together about buying a home
> - a. research mortgage options
> - b. apply for first-time home buyers' program
> - c. look at different neighborhoods, check out school districts
> - d. teach kids about importance of owning a home
>
> Supporting Idea 2: Reduce our expenses
> - a. join warehouse club for groceries
> - b. save on vacations by staying with family or doing things at home
> - c. don't eat out, even fast food is expensive for a family
> - d. no paid babysitters or full-price movies

You can see Marc's original brainstormed list on page 43. Right now, spend a few minutes comparing that list with the outline above. What differences do you notice?

_____

_____

You probably noticed that the original brainstormed list has no order, but that the outline is organized. You probably also noticed that the brainstormed list contains ideas that don't relate to the thesis. As Marc focused his supporting ideas, he left those out of the outline.

Writing a First Draft

Dorothy and Marc are now both ready for the next step in the writing process. They can write a **first draft**. As they write this first version, they will turn their ideas into sentences. They will turn groups of ideas into paragraphs.

As you write your first draft, try not to listen to the "editor" or "critic" voice in your head. Tell that voice to be quiet. Its turn will come later. In the first draft, your writer voice has to take over and get the job done.

Have you ever stopped writing because you couldn't spell a word? Or because you weren't sure about a comma? In your first draft, spell the word as best you can. Put in a comma—you can take it out later. Just let the writer voice flow through your fingers.

THE WRITING PROCESS ▪ PRACTICE 4

A. Review the list you brainstormed on page 43 in Practice 1. You wrote down a goal and brainstormed ways to achieve it. Follow the steps below to create an outline.

1. Write a thesis statement for a piece of writing based on your list. Remember, the thesis is the main point you want to make about the topic—your goal and how you might achieve it.

   Thesis statement:

   _____

   _____

2. Evaluate the ideas on your list. Cross out ideas that don't relate to the thesis.

3. See how some ideas are related to each other. Write a supporting idea that tells how they are related. Then list them under the supporting idea. If you think of other good ideas, add them. (Use another sheet of paper if you need more space.)

   Supporting Idea 1:

   _____

   _____

   _____

   Supporting Idea 2:

   _____

   _____

   _____

B. Now write a first draft:
   ▪ Start with your thesis statement.
   ▪ Write a paragraph about each supporting idea and its details.
   You can work from the outline you just made and write about your goal. Or you can work from the picture you created on page 47 and write about a person. It's up to you. Which one does your writer voice like better? Write that one!

Keep your first draft. You will work on it further in the next section.

Feedback and models start on page 179.
For more practice with outlining, see page 145.

"Over time, revision just becomes part of the process of writing.... And you get better at it!"

Revising and Editing

How to Read Your Own Writing

After you've written a first draft, the next step in the writing process is improving it. To improve a draft, first read it over with an open mind. Good writers use two important strategies for reading their own writing:

- **Set your writing aside for a while.** It's not helpful to read something you've just written. You can't think of how to change it. It needs to rest. (So do you!)

- **Read your writing out loud.** Reading out loud helps you experience the words on the paper fully. You can also hear how they sound. When you read silently, you skip along too quickly.

Has your writing rested for a day or so since you wrote a draft in Practice 4, page 49? Are you ready to read your draft out loud? Try it now.

How do you feel about this piece of writing now? What do you think about it? What changes would you like to make? Write your thoughts below.

_____

_____

_____

Revising a Draft

When you **revise**, you look at two aspects of your writing:

- the content—the thesis, supporting ideas, and details
- the organization—the order of ideas and paragraphs

Look at how Marc revised a paragraph from his first draft about buying a home. Here's the paragraph:

> First we can start learning about buying a home. My wife and I will learn about different types of mortgages. We can drive around a few different neighborhoods to see what the homes are like. We'll also talk to everyone we know about the schools in those areas. We are going to teach the kids about the importance of owning a home. We want them to understand why we all have to work hard on this goal.

Marc reread the third and fourth sentences. He thought they related to a different supporting idea than the other sentences. He also wanted to write more about the different neighborhoods his family would explore. So Marc decided to divide this paragraph. He circled the two sentences and moved them to start a new paragraph.

Do major revisions first. Then see what minor revisions are needed. For example, if you decide to develop a new supporting idea, you might break a paragraph in two, as Marc did. Then you would make some changes to each of the new paragraphs.

Revising on a Computer

Have you ever heard of **cut and paste**? On a computer, you can move words from one spot ("cut" them) and place them somewhere else ("paste" them). Marc could cut those two sentences out of his paragraph and paste them below it, creating a new paragraph.

Many writers feel that computers make revising easier. You might agree. If you can, experiment with using a computer for revision.

 THE WRITING PROCESS ▪ PRACTICE 5

A. Read your first draft aloud again. Think about how you could improve the content and the organization. Your notes on page 50 can help you get started. Make a plan for revising your draft by answering these questions.

   1. Improving the Content

      a. Is your thesis stated clearly? If not, how could you improve it?

      _____

      b. Can you add more supporting ideas? Are there any ideas that don't belong?

      _____

   2. Improving the Organization

      a. Does the order of your ideas make sense? If not, how could you change it?

      _____

      b. Do all the ideas in each paragraph belong? Should you divide a paragraph?

      _____

B. Now revise your draft. Use the editing marks shown on page 191 in the Handbook to move, add, and delete ideas.

    Keep your revised draft. You will work on it further in the next section.

Feedback starts on page 179.
For more practice with editing, see page 146.

Editing a Draft

On the video, you heard about the important difference between revising and editing. Revising comes first. You want to be confident that your ideas are expressed clearly and strongly. Then you can start editing.

When you **edit**, you correct mistakes in word choice, grammar, punctuation, spelling, and capitalization. These things may seem little or unimportant, but they can leave a bad impression. They can also interfere with getting your message across.

As you work through this book, you'll learn more about editing. You'll see how to spot and correct the kinds of errors that many writers make. For now, focus on three steps in editing your writing:

1. **Read your writing out loud.** (Does this sound familiar?) Your ear sometimes can hear mistakes that your eyes don't notice.

2. **Check for the errors you make most often.** Most writers make the same mistakes over and over.

3. **As a beginning editor, ask someone else to help you edit.** Most writers have a hard time seeing their own mistakes. Someone else can help you spot yours. That will help you with step 2.

Marc has revised his essay. He has edited the first paragraph. Note the mistakes he corrected. What kind of mistake did Marc make the most?

My whole family can work together to ~~acheive~~ *achieve* our goal of buying a home. First we ~~can~~ start learning about buying a home. My wife and I will learn about ~~diffrent~~ *different* types of mortgages. Mary can go on the Internet, she will look for information about a first-time home buyers' program. We will also teach the kids about the ~~importence~~ *importance* of owning a home. We want them to understand why we all have to work hard on this goal.

Marc inserted one missing verb and fixed one error in sentence structure. However, he corrected *three* misspelled words. Spelling poses a special problem for him, so he looks carefully for spelling errors when he edits.

Edit Marc's second paragraph at the top of the next page. Read it aloud if you can. Try to hear any errors. Have someone help you spot errors if you like.

Circle any mistakes you find. Then use the editing marks shown on page 191 to correct the mistakes.

> We will drive around a few diffrent neighborhoods to see what the
>
> homes are like. We'll talk to everyone we know about the schools in those
>
> areas. My children have very strong feelings about this, they want to live in
>
> Bridgewater. Their is a new middel school and a public pool.

Did you see that Marc separated two sentences with just a comma? The sentences should be written this way: "My children have very strong feelings about this. They want to live in Bridgewater."

If spelling is not a problem for you, you may have found three misspelled words: *different, There,* and *middle.* It helps to know what kind of mistakes to look for.

Target Error List

Most writers know the mistakes they tend to make. Maybe you have trouble with spelling, or maybe commas give you a headache. Think about your own writing. List three or four errors to look out for—to "take aim at"—when you edit.

_____

_____

THE WRITING PROCESS ▪ PRACTICE 6

Now try the three-step editing strategy on your own writing. Use your Target Error List from above too. Get out your revised draft from Practice 5, page 51, and follow these steps.

1. Read your writing aloud. Circle errors you hear as you read. When you're finished, go back and correct the errors you circled. Practice using the editing marks.

2. Check for the errors on your Target Error List. Fix any mistakes you find.

3. Ask someone else to help you edit. If this person finds any new errors, are they the same type of errors you have found?

When you're finished, revisit your Target Error List. Do you need to make any changes? If so, make them.

Save your edited draft. You will put it in the portfolio you make in the next section.

Feedback starts on page 179.

For more practice with editing, see page 146.

Making a Portfolio

Have you ever heard of an artist's portfolio? Artists use portfolios to organize their pictures. They show their portfolios to employers, customers, and other artists.

Just like artists, writers may have portfolios of their works. You can make a portfolio to hold the writing that you do for this book. Some of the pieces that you write will go through several drafts. Your portfolio will help you organize your drafts as well as share your final draft with others. From time to time, review all the work in your portfolio. You'll see how your writing has improved!

Your **portfolio** is an organized collection of your writing. For one assignment, it may include several drafts as well as your final draft.

Instructions for Making a Portfolio

1. Get a folder that has two inside pockets.
2. Write your name on the front. If you are working in a classroom, write your teacher's name in the lower right-hand corner.
3. If you like, decorate the front in any way that represents you. You might draw something or glue on a picture—a personal photo or a cutout from a magazine.
4. On the inside, label the left pocket *Works in Progress*. Label the right pocket *Final Works with Drafts*.

When you are through, your portfolio will look something like this:

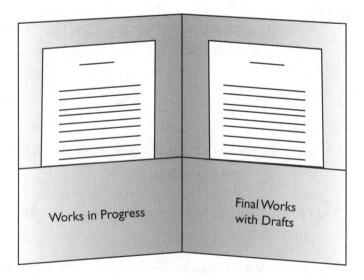

In this book, you will sometimes see the picture to the right next to a writing assignment. When you see that picture, put your work for that assignment in your writing portfolio. Include the date on it.

The best way to start practicing to write is the writing assessment below. It will help you see how you feel about writing. It will also show you what kinds of writing you already do and what kinds you want to practice.

1. Follow the instructions on page 54 to make a portfolio.

2. Fill in the chart below. Then copy your answers on a sheet of paper with your name at the top. Include the date. Make this the first page of your portfolio.

Read each statement. Check whether it is always, sometimes, or never true.

	Always	Sometimes	Never
I like to write.			
I feel I write fairly well.			
I can get enough ideas to write about.			
People are interested in what I write about.			
People can understand what I'm writing about.			
My grammar is good.			
My spelling is correct.			
My punctuation is correct.			

Read each statement. Check whether it is always, sometimes, or never true.

Kind of Writing	I can write this fairly well.	I want to improve this.	I want to learn how to write this.	I don't want to learn to write this.
E-mail message				
Personal letter				
Business letter				
Poem				
Personal story				
Essay				

For example: *Julia Sanchez Writing Self-Assessment*

> I sometimes like to write.
> I can write personal letters and poems fairly well.
> I want to improve writing personal stories.
> I want to learn to write essays and business letters.
> I don't want to learn to write e-mail.

3. Put your revised and edited draft about a goal you have or an important person in your life into your portfolio.

GED ESSAY CONNECTION

Responding to the Topic

On the GED Test, you will be asked to write an essay in response to a topic. Before you begin work on your essay, read the topic carefully. It will tell you what to write about in your essay. Your essay score depends partly on how well you stick to the topic.

Earlier in this lesson, you learned that a thesis is the point a writer wants to make about a topic. For your GED essay, your thesis will be the point you want to make about the assigned topic.

Read the following topic carefully. It is similar to many topics used on the GED Test.

TOPIC

How has television influenced you and your life?

In your essay, explain your answer with examples from your personal knowledge, observations, and experience.

Notice that this topic contains a question. One way to help you respond is to write that question *to yourself* at the top of your paper: **How has television influenced me and my life?** Underline the key words so that they stand out: *television, influenced,* and *life.* Think of them as you brainstorm or cluster ideas for your essay.

Once you've gotten ideas, write your thesis statement. Then reread the topic question. Does your thesis statement answer the topic question? If so, you're on the right track.

Monika, who is preparing for the GED Test, is working on this topic for practice. She brainstormed a list of ideas. Then she wrote this thesis statement:

> *I feel that television has been a good influence in my life because I watch mostly shows that are good for me.*

Does her thesis respond to the topic? Yes. Basically, it answers "good influence" to the question *How has television influenced you and your life?* On her list, she should keep the ideas that support the good influence of TV. She should delete those that don't. That will help her score high on responding to the topic.

Patrick made a cluster of ideas and then wrote this thesis statement. Does it respond to the topic?

> *I watch a lot of good television shows.*

No, that thesis statement does not really respond to the topic. It does not answer the question *how* at all.

How would you respond to that topic? Take a few minutes to get some ideas on another sheet of paper. Then write a thesis statement here.

_____

Read your thesis. Does it answer the topic question?

 You will use your thesis statement and your brainstormed list later.

GED ESSAY PRACTICE

RESPOND TO THE TOPIC

Read the topic below.

TOPIC

Choose a person who you think is a hero.

In your essay, explain why that person is a hero. Support your essay with your own experiences, knowledge, and observations.

I. The topic is not in the form of a question. Choose a person to write about. Then rewrite the topic as a question to yourself below. Underline the key words.

_____

2. Now brainstorm for three minutes to get ideas about the topic.

_____

_____

_____

_____

_____

_____

_____

3. Write a thesis statement here. Then check to see if your statement responds to the topic.

_____

Feedback starts on page 179.
For more practice with responding to the topic, see page 147.

GED Review: The Writing Process

Reread this example of a topic you might find on the GED Writing Test.

GED REVIEW

> ## TOPIC
>
> How has television influenced you and your life?
>
> In your essay, explain your answer with examples from your personal knowledge, observations, and experience.

A. Evaluate ideas.

1. Below are the thesis statement and brainstormed list that Monika, the GED student, prepared. Read them carefully. What ideas should Monika delete from her list because they do not support her thesis statement? Cross them out.

   Thesis: I feel that television has been a good influence in my life because I mainly watch shows that are good for me.

   > watch movies like <u>Glory</u> based on inspiring stories
   > learn from history programs
   > learn from Biography channel
   > learn from science programs
   > cable has many different kinds of channels
   > sometimes tape soap operas
   > TV comedies can be good for relaxing and relieving stress
   > watch GED prep programs on public TV
   > enjoy watching cartoons with my son and laughing
   > Kenny wants me to watch sports with him
   > too much football on TV for me
   > Olympic Games and athletes inspire me

2. Organize Monika's ideas. Write each remaining idea under the appropriate label of the supporting idea.

   TV Shows Educate   **TV Shows Help Relax**   **TV Shows Inspire**

   _____   _____   _____

   _____   _____   _____

B. Evaluate and organize your own ideas.

1. Go back to your thesis on page 57 and your own brainstormed list. Cross out any
    ideas you don't want to keep. Add ideas if you can.

2. Organize your ideas.

    a. Group related ideas. You can circle related ideas or rewrite them in a list.

    b. Give each group a label that tells the supporting idea. You should come up with
        at least two supporting ideas.

    Supporting Idea 1: _____   **Supporting Idea 2:** _____

    _____   _____

    _____   _____

    _____   _____

    _____   _____

3. Draw a picture here of your thesis statement and supporting ideas. You can use a
    table with supporting legs or any other picture that works well for you.

C. Write about the topic.

Take your organized notes and write two or three paragraphs on the assigned topic.
Use the Writing Process in the Handbook on page 190 to help you follow the
remaining steps.

Now spend a few minutes thinking about how the Writing Process steps are working
to help you write. Check which strategies seem to work best for you.

❑ Brainstorming

❑ Clustering

❑ Picturing

❑ Outlining

❑ Reading aloud

❑ Target Error List

Feedback starts on page 179.

Organized Writing

1. Think About the Topic

You are about to watch a program on *Organized Writing*. This video explains the importance of putting your thoughts in a clear and logical order.

In this video you will see professional writers, writing teachers, and students discuss different ways of organizing your thoughts. One writer will use the example of being in a grocery store and knowing where you will find the milk. How is this example like well-organized writing?

2. Prepare to Watch the Video

Several people in this program discuss using details to "show" something rather than tell about it. Pick a favorite possession of yours. Write a few sentences that would "show" it to a reader:

_____

_____

_____

Here's an example of writing that "shows." Is your writing similar? *One of the buttons is missing—right in the middle. It used to be bright red and black, but the colors are now faded and dull. The tattered hole in the back isn't too noticeable. My wife calls it "that rag," but I feel more at home in my old flannel shirt than anything else.*

3. Preview the Questions

Read the questions under *Think About the Program* on the next page and keep them in mind as you watch the program. After you watch, use the questions to review the main ideas in the program.

4. Study the Vocabulary

Review the terms to the right. Understanding the meaning of writing vocabulary will help you understand the video and the rest of the lesson.

WATCH THE PROGRAM

As you watch the program, pay special attention to the host who introduces or summarizes major ideas that you need to learn about. The host will also tell you important information about the GED Writing Test.

AFTER YOU WATCH

1. Think About the Program

Why is organization in a piece of writing important?

In writing, what is the difference between telling your readers something and "showing" them something?

What are some different methods you can use to organize your writing?

How does asking yourself questions such as *How? Why? Who?* and *Who says?* help strengthen your writing?

2. Make the Connection

Think of the three methods of organization discussed in the video: sequence of events, compare and contrast, and cause and effect. Have you ever used these methods to organize information in your daily life?

TERMS

compare and contrast— to show how two or more things are alike and different

conclusion—an ending paragraph that sums up what an essay was about

flow—to lead logically and smoothly from one sentence to the next

introduction—an opening paragraph that tells a reader what an essay will be about

paragraph—a group of sentences about one main idea

pros and cons—reasons for and against something

sequence—time order; the order in which events happen

supporting sentences— sentences in a paragraph that explain the point in the topic sentence

topic sentence—a sentence in a paragraph that tells what the main idea is

transition words—words or phrases that signal a reader how ideas are related or what is to come

"When you start writing, determine a lead—a first, beginning sentence—that summarizes what you're going to say or prepares your reader for where you're going."

Writing Topic Sentences

How Does a Paragraph Work?

A **paragraph** is a group of sentences about one main idea. When you read, you can spot a paragraph easily. The first line may be indented (beginning a little to the right of the others). Otherwise, space separates the paragraph from other paragraphs, like the paragraphs on this page. When you write, be sure to indent each of your paragraphs.

Readers expect each paragraph to stick to one idea. A paragraph usually contains a **topic sentence** that tells what that main idea is. The rest of the sentences support, or explain, the topic sentence.

There's no rule about how long a paragraph should be. Yet think about how long *you* like a paragraph to be when you're reading—not too long, right? Four to six sentences is a good length. A paragraph is a "bite-sized" chunk of writing.

A Good Topic Sentence Clues the Reader

Writers often place a topic sentence at the beginning of a paragraph. In that position, it lets the reader know up front what to expect. For example, look at Luis's funny story about taking his children swimming. His topic sentences are underlined. After each topic sentence, the rest of the paragraph tells you more about that main idea.

Going to the Pool

Have you ever taken three children to the pool? It sounds easy. However, let me tell you what it's really like.

<u>First, I have to get everything ready.</u> My wife is so helpful. She gives me a list of 73 things to take with me. Each kid also must take 27 special toys and other items. I fill every tote bag in the house, but I forget the towels. Oops.

<u>When we arrive at the pool, we need to change into our suits.</u> The girls go into the women's showers by themselves. Will they ever come out? I wonder. My son and I are out of the showers in an instant. We are ready to go. We wait and wait and wait for the girls. . . .

<u>The next step is to put on the sunscreen.</u> Do you know how much a little boy can wiggle? He has sunscreen in his eyes and hair by the time I'm done. The girls refuse to let me help them. I say then they better do a good job! They are sassy. "We know how to do it, Dad. We're not babies."

<u>Finally, it's time to swim.</u> Ready, set, jump in!

Luis used **sequence,** or time order, to organize his story. Notice how each paragraph starts at a new point in time. Each topic sentence identifies the next point in time.

In the video, you saw how **transition words** help show sequence. Luis's topic sentences contain some common transition words—*first, when, next,* and *finally.* Circle those words in Luis's topic sentences. Can you see how they are signals for you, the reader?

Other transition time words include the following:

once   then   before   after   in the beginning   in the end

ORGANIZED WRITING ▪ PRACTICE 1

A. The story below is missing some topic sentences. Read the whole story first. Then, on each line, write a topic sentence for the paragraph that follows. Your topic sentence should clue a reader to what the paragraph is about. Use some transition time words if you can. The first one has been done as an example.

The Big Game

We're going to the Gray Sox game—Rosie, George, Noah, and me. We've got our tickets and made our plans. Now it's the big night.

At first, it seems like it's all about just getting there.

We meet at the train station. We have to take a train from the west side to downtown. Then we change trains to get to the ballpark. It takes a long time. It's crowded. We can't get seats together on the train.

_____

People are streaming along all the sidewalks. We find the right gate, then we manage to find our seats. We settle in and argue about who will go get hot dogs.

_____

Frank Bellini hits a home run, his first time up at bat! The crowd goes wild. It's a good game. We forget about the hot dogs and root for our team.

_____

The Stars are ahead. But the Stars pitcher walks two batters in a row. Sox fans are screaming. The next batter is Loren Malteez. He hits a double, brings in one run. Now the score is tied.

It's anybody's game until the ninth inning. The Stars don't score in the top. We're at bat in the bottom of the ninth. Sammy Romer hits the second home run of the night, and the game is ours!

B. Think about this topic: *what I did last Sunday afternoon.* On a separate sheet of paper, list three to five ideas about that topic. Then write a topic sentence for a paragraph about the topic.

Writing models start on page 180.

Be Specific, but Not Too Specific!

A good topic sentence tells what's coming up in a paragraph. If a topic sentence is too general, the reader won't know the main *point* of the paragraph. If it is too specific, the reader won't know what to expect from the *whole* paragraph.

Like the students in the video program, Richard is writing about credit cards. In his paragraph below, he explains why he likes credit cards. He signals that point in his topic sentence:

> <u>In my experience, credit cards are useful.</u> You can pay for almost anything with a credit card. Too many businesses don't like to take checks. I don't like to carry a lot of cash with me. So I carry my credit card.

Shakeena is also writing about credit cards. Here's a topic sentence from one of her paragraphs:

> I have a credit card.

Do you have an idea of what Shakeena will say next? No. Her topic sentence is too general. She hasn't told you her specific point about credit cards in that sentence. Now read the rest of the paragraph. Can you think of a better topic sentence?

> When I first got my credit card, I was careful about not charging too much stuff. But then my sister had a baby. I wanted to help her. I bought dozens of baby things on my credit card—clothes, diapers, a crib, a stroller. I'm still paying for them. That baby is almost a year old now!

Which of these statements would be a good topic sentence for that paragraph?

☐   I have charged baby things on my credit card.

☐   I have learned that it's easy to spend too much with a credit card.

The first statement is too specific. Shakeena does mention charging things for a baby. However, that is not the main point of her paragraph. It is only part of her explanation.

The second statement is a good topic sentence for the paragraph. It tells you the main point of the paragraph. It lets you know what will follow—Shakeena's bad experience with a credit card. It is not too general. It is not too specific.

A. Revise another topic sentence that is too general. Here is another paragraph from Shakeena's essay. The topic sentence is underlined. Write a more specific topic sentence on the lines below the paragraph. Tell a reader what Shakeena's point is.

<u>My friend Anna got a credit card too.</u> She didn't think about how she would pay the bill. She figured her parents would help her. Her boyfriend owed her money, and she thought she could use that too. But her parents refused to help, and her boyfriend never paid her. Anna has a huge bill every month, and it's all up to her to pay it. If she doesn't make payments, she'll get a bad credit rating.

_____

_____

B. Tomas's essay below is missing some topic sentences. Read the whole essay first. Then write topic sentences where they are needed. Remember that a topic sentence should help lead the reader into the paragraph. It should be specific, but not too specific.

The Way to Use Credit Cards

Let me share my experience with credit cards. I hope you can learn from it. Be careful how you use them!

_____

All kinds of businesses take credit cards. I can order over the phone or on the Internet with my credit card. I can even charge movie tickets and popcorn at the refreshment counter. I almost never have to have cash or write a check.

_____

One day I buy groceries. The next day it's new shoes and shin guards so my daughter can play soccer. Then I need a new bus pass to get to work. By the end of one week, I don't even remember all the things we paid for with our card.

I have learned to save all the receipts in one place. I count them up every week. I make sure that we will be able to pay the whole bill every month! That's the best way to use a credit card.

C. Check the topic sentence you wrote about your Sunday afternoon for Practice 1 on page 63. Is it too general or too specific? If so, revise it.

Writing models start on page 180.
For more practice with topic sentences, see page 148.

"Make sure each sentence within a paragraph relates to the point of the paragraph. And make sure the supporting information you use is detailed and specific."

Writing Paragraphs

Supporting the Topic Sentence

After the topic sentence in a paragraph comes the nitty-gritty. The sentences that follow the topic sentence help explain it. Because they support the point in the topic sentence, they are called supporting details or **supporting sentences.**

Read Marcia's paragraph about her moving day. See how each sentence adds a new detail to support the idea in the topic sentence:

> <u>When Howard showed up with the truck at 8 A.M., we were not ready!</u> I was still packing dishes. Max was trying to catch the cat in the back yard. Laura refused to put her stuffed animals in a box because then they wouldn't be able to breathe.

Each supporting sentence shows one way that the family was not ready to move. The topic sentence makes you expect these details. The supporting sentences provide the kinds of details a reader expects.

Should Marcia add a sentence to this paragraph describing her new home? Check one:

☐ Yes, it *would* support the topic sentence.

☐ No, it would *not* support the topic sentence.

The answer is no. The topic sentence is about not being ready to move. The family's new home has nothing to do with that idea.

Ideas That Flow

Sentences in a paragraph should flow. **Flow** means that the ideas lead logically from one sentence to the next. The reader can follow the ideas.

Here is another paragraph from Marcia's moving day story. See how Marcia's writing helps move you, the reader, from one idea to the next:

> <u>Finally, we began to pack the truck.</u> First, we made a wall of boxes up to the roof of the truck. Then we loaded the big furniture—the mattresses, couch, and dining room table. Next was smaller furniture. We fit bicycles, lamps, and other awkward things in last. As we went along, we padded all the corners and edges.

Did you notice the transition words, like *First* and *Then*? These words help you follow Marcia's story. Circle all the words and phrases that help the flow.

Did you circle *next, last*, and *as we went along?*

Now you know what makes an organized paragraph:

- a topic sentence
- supporting sentences
- a flow of ideas

ORGANIZED WRITING ▪ PRACTICE 3

A. Cortney wrote to a friend about his chef training program. Here are two paragraphs from his letter.

1. Underline the topic sentence in each paragraph.

2. Circle any word or phrase that helps the sentences flow.

3. Cross out a sentence that does not support the topic sentence of its paragraph.

Every cooking class follows the same pattern. The teacher starts with a demonstration of a cooking skill, like making pastry. Light pastry is very hard to make. Then we study a recipe together, and we talk about planning the steps in the recipe. Next, we prepare by getting out the ingredients and tools we need. Finally, we work in teams to make the dish. The teacher checks each team's work at the end.

Last week, I learned a big lesson about cakes. At first, I didn't understand why we were supposed to beat the batter for so long. Then I saw the difference in the cakes. The team next to us had this perfect, light cake. But ours was kind of flat and tough. When the teacher came around, she said we didn't beat enough air into the batter.

B. Now it's your turn to write an organized paragraph. Here is your topic: Write about a time you learned something. It could be a specific skill, or it could be a lesson in life.

To write your paragraph, use what you have learned. On a separate sheet of paper, follow these steps:

❑ With your reader in mind, make a list or cluster of ideas.

❑ Write a topic sentence. Your topic sentence should tell the reader what to expect in your paragraph.

❑ Write 3 to 5 supporting sentences, based on your list or cluster. Try to use transitions to signal the flow of ideas to your reader.

❑ Wait for a few hours or overnight.

❑ Review your paragraph. If you can add details, do so. If you can add transitions, do so. If any sentences don't support your topic sentence, cross them out.

Answers and feedback start on page 180.

Organizing Ideas

Sequence is one way to organize ideas. You also saw in the video other ways to organize ideas when you write.

PROS AND CONS. For example, one class wrote about the pros and cons of credit cards. You might, like Richard on page 64, write just about the pros of an issue. You might, like Shakeena, write just about the cons. But you can also, like Tomas on page 65, write about both pros and cons.

Barney is writing a letter to his nephew, Will. Barney has been in the army, and Will is thinking about enlisting. Barney does not want to tell his nephew what to do. He wants to show Will both sides of basic training so that Will can decide for himself:

> <u>Many new recruits worry about getting through basic training.</u> I have to be honest, Will, it's really hard. You're far from home, and you're always exhausted. The sergeants are hard on you, and the food is terrible. On the other hand, you learn a lot. You find out about yourself, and you make friends like you've never had before.

The first part of the paragraph tells the cons of basic training. The second part tells the pros. Underline the phrase *On the other hand*. That is where the ideas shift. Could you tell that as a reader?

COMPARE AND CONTRAST. Writers also often make comparisons. In the video, a teacher made a comparison between *Romeo and Juliet* and *West Side Story*. A comparison shows what's alike and what's different between two or more things.

For example, Leah is writing to her father about her sons. Here is one of her paragraphs:

> Andy and Michael are both in middle school now. They start off every morning with their backpacks crammed with books and projects. Michael organizes all his stuff neatly. He knows exactly when his assignments are due. But Andy is always winging it. He takes school one day at a time, and every day is a panic! I try to help him plan ahead, but it's a battle.

Can you see how Leah organized her paragraph? Underline the sentences that describe both boys. The other sentences describe only Michael or only Andy. Circle a word that alerts the reader to a shift from one boy to the other in the middle of the paragraph.

Did you underline the first two sentences and circle the word *But?*

Writers use many different transitions to signal shifts in their ideas. You probably have seen the ones below. Practice using these signals in your own writing:

on the other hand   *in contrast*   *but*   *nevertheless*   *however*

A. Write a pro/con paragraph, like the one Barney wrote to Will. Here is your topic: Describe something that has both good points and bad points. It could be a movie, marriage, money, or anything else. Use the checklist below to help you plan, draft, and revise your paragraph.

_____

_____

_____

_____

_____

_____

B. Write a compare/contrast paragraph, like Leah's paragraph about her sons. Here is your topic: Compare and contrast two people who are partly alike and partly different. Use the checklist below to help you plan, draft, and revise your paragraph.

_____

_____

_____

_____

_____

_____

WRITING CHECKLIST

To write each paragraph, follow these steps:

❏ With your reader in mind, make a list or cluster of ideas on a separate sheet of paper.

❏ Write a topic sentence on the first line for the paragraph above. Your topic sentence should tell the reader what to expect in your paragraph.

❏ Write 3 to 5 supporting sentences, based on your list or cluster. Try to use transitions to signal the flow of ideas to your reader.

❏ Wait for a few hours or overnight.

❏ Review your paragraph. If you can add details, do so. If you can add transitions, do so. If any sentences don't support your topic sentence, cross them out.

❏ Copy your revised paragraph on a sheet of paper, and put it in your portfolio.

Feedback starts on page 180.
For more practice with organizing paragraphs, see page 149.

"When you're looking at a document that's well organized, things don't come out of left field. They belong. Ideas stay together."

Dividing and Combining Paragraphs

Dividing a Paragraph

Sometimes you start with one idea, and that idea leads to another idea. Before you know it, you've got a page of writing—but it's all one paragraph! One long paragraph is hard to read.

Look at an example:

Everyday Art and Everyday Artists

      I believe that almost everybody is an artist in his or her own way. I see examples of everyday art all around me. Children draw pictures on the sidewalk with chalk. My mother brings over her scrapbooking. My dad makes his own fishing flies. Matty stencils a pattern on the wall in his bedroom—in nonwashable paint. People think that because someone gave them a pattern and they didn't make it up themselves, it's not art. Well, it's still art. If you make something yourself, you put something of yourself into it. You made your own version of it. It doesn't matter if someone else created the stencil you started with. We have to teach kids to think of the things they create as art. If we don't, then they won't realize that they are artists. They'll grow up thinking that art is something that someone else makes.

As Chondra wrote about art, her ideas grew! Now she needs to revise her writing. She needs to make three paragraphs. That way, readers like you can find her three main points more easily.

Read Chondra's paragraph again. Where are two places where she could divide the paragraph?

Chondra made paragraph marks (like this: ¶) before "People think that. . . ." and "We have to teach kids. . . ."

Writing New Topic Sentences

Dividing a paragraph often means that your new paragraphs need a little work.

Look at Chondra's revision on the next page. She has added a topic sentence for her new second paragraph. She also changed the beginning of the next sentence.

Everyday Art and Everyday Artists

I believe that almost everybody is an artist in his or her own way. I see examples of everyday art all around me. Children draw pictures on the sidewalk with chalk. My mother brings over her scrapbooking. My dad makes his own fishing flies. Matty stencils a pattern on the wall in his bedroom—in nonwashable paint.

<u>However, people don't realize that they make art all the time. They</u> think that because someone gave them a pattern and they didn't make it up themselves, it's not art. Well, it's still art. If you make something yourself, you put something of yourself into it. You made your own version of it. It doesn't matter if someone else created the stencil you started with.

We have to teach kids to think of the things they create as art. If we don't, then they won't realize that they are artists. They'll grow up thinking that art is something that someone else makes.

ORGANIZED WRITING ▪ PRACTICE 5

A. Revise the paragraph below by dividing it into three paragraphs. Use the paragraph mark. One of the new paragraphs will need a topic sentence. Write a good topic sentence in the margin, and show where it belongs with an arrow.

My First Job

Most people remember their first job. Like a lot of people, I got my first job in fast food. It paid minimum wage. It was fun at first. But after a while, I saw that every shift was the same. It was not an exciting job, and it never would be. One of the managers had gone to school for many years, and he could speak Russian. I'll never know how he ended up managing a burger joint. There were other talented people too. Theresa was too good at math to spend her career counting out four pickle slices per burger. John talked about all the books he read and how he was writing a mystery novel. At the time, I couldn't understand why these people stayed in their jobs. But that was 25 years ago, and I'm wiser now. I know that there are lots of problems that hold people back. Being "smart" isn't important. You have to have a certain drive. You can't be afraid of hard work or of a challenge. It helps to have support from your family and friends to make something out of your life. And you have to stay out of trouble.

B. Check your portfolio for writing with long paragraphs. See if you can find at least one paragraph that could be divided.

❑ Mark the places where you would divide the paragraph.

❑ Move or delete sentences if it will improve your writing.

❑ Make sure each new paragraph has a good topic sentence.

Answers and writing models start on page 181.
For more practice with dividing paragraphs, see page 150.

WRITING SKILLS

Combining Paragraphs

When you revise, you may see a connection that you didn't see before. The ideas in two *different* paragraphs may actually support the *same* main idea. In that case, the two paragraphs really should be just one.

Look at an example. Lonnie is writing a memo to the limo drivers in his company:

RED LINE LIMO

MEMO

To: All Drivers of Red Line Limo
From: Lonnie
Subject: Customer relations

Last night, one of our drivers was late picking up a customer. Traffic was unusually heavy to begin with. Then a backup from an accident really delayed him.

When the customer was dropped off, he wanted a huge discount. The driver got into a shouting match with him.

Eventually, the customer gave in and paid. Of course, the driver didn't get any tip!

In the future, if this happens to you, first tell the customer you're sorry! Explain why you are late. Customers have a right to expect on-time service.

Then follow this procedure: Tell the customer that only management can give a discount, and have the customer call the office.

If Jake or I are here, we'll probably give a discount. If we're not here, say you will talk to management about refunding part of the charge. In the meantime, give the customer one of our $3.00 off coupons good for his NEXT ride with us!

The paragraphs in Lonnie's memo are short and choppy. It's difficult to understand the connection between ideas. The reader has to work too hard to understand!

Lonnie revised his memo. He saw that the second and third paragraphs should actually be one. Both tell what happened when the customer was dropped off. So Lonnie made a mark like this to show the paragraphs should be run together:

When the customer was dropped off, he wanted a huge discount. The driver got into a shouting match with him.

Eventually, the customer gave in and paid. Of course, the driver didn't get any tip!

Can you see another place where two paragraphs should be combined? Draw a line to show the combination.

You may have seen that the last two paragraphs should be combined. Both tell what to do to get a discount.

When you combine paragraphs, you may need to revise the topic sentence. You may also need to make other changes. The whole new paragraph should flow for your reader.

ORGANIZED WRITING ▪ PRACTICE 6

A. **Some paragraphs in this story should be combined. Read carefully. Decide the best way to combine them and rewrite the story below. Indent each paragraph you write. Make sure each paragraph has a good topic sentence.**

Many people think that working at home is easy. But when I got a job stuffing envelopes at home, it was not easy for me.

I thought I wanted to work at home. I could set my own hours. I would not have to take the bus to work.

I would also save money on work clothes and lunches.

However, I did not have a good place to work in the apartment. It was hard to put in enough hours. My family distracted me.

My boss told me that I had to produce more. Otherwise, he would have to let me go. Then he fired me.

At first I was very angry with myself. Yet I did learn something from the experience. I got a job in a supermarket, and I love taking the bus every day!

_____

_____

_____

_____

_____

_____

_____

B. **Check your portfolio for writing with paragraphs that should be combined.**

❏ Mark the paragraphs to show how you would combine them.

❏ Move or delete sentences if it will improve your writing.

❏ Make sure each new paragraph has a good topic sentence.

Answers and writing models start on page 181.
For more practice with combining paragraphs, see page 150.

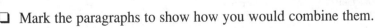

WRITING SKILLS

Using Organizers

In the video, you saw a drawing of a "guiding hand." It helped a writer organize his writing and stay on track. Writers have invented many such tools to help them think and organize. In earlier programs you learned about some others. Now try these two tools to help you.

Charts

A chart can help you think of pros and cons—reasons for and against something. For example, Rana was writing an essay about a decision she had to make. She was deciding whether to buy a car. She made a two-column chart. Then she listed the pros and cons:

Yes, I should	No, I should not
easier and freer to go places	Costs an awful lot—would go in debt
can drive to a better job	would have to buy used—may get lemon
would be more popular!	hidden expenses—like insurance

The chart helped Rana think of ideas. It also helped her organize them. She wrote one paragraph about why she should buy a car. Then she wrote one paragraph about why she shouldn't. In the end, the chart also helped Rana make up her mind. She decided not to buy a car for a while.

Venn Diagrams

A Venn diagram has two overlapping circles. It can help you compare and contrast. For example, Brad was writing a comparison of basketball and hockey. In the left circle, he wrote details about only basketball. In the right circle he put details about only hockey. In the overlapping middle area, Brad listed details that both sports share:

Basketball   **Hockey**

played on a court — five men play — played on ice

no special protection — score into a net — special equipment — sticks, gloves, and padding

— drop back on defense —

one player can dominate — fast breaks — fast

— fakes —

finesse – quickness of players — winter games played into the summer! — violent

A Venn diagram can also help you discover a new connection. For example, Ted is writing about working toward his GED. He wants to write about how his reading and writing have improved. Is there a hidden relationship between these two? He uses a Venn diagram to help him think:

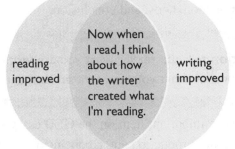

reading improved

Now when I read, I think about how the writer created what I'm reading.

writing improved

At first Ted labeled only the two main circles. Then he thought about what the middle area might mean. His diagram helped him come up with a very insightful idea!

USING THE WRITER'S TOOL ■ USE AN ORGANIZER

A. **Use the chart below. List the pros and cons of people using cell phones.**

Or, if you prefer, think of a personal decision you must make. Use the chart to list pros and cons. It might help you decide!

PROS	CONS

B. **On a separate sheet of paper, draw a Venn diagram. Label the left circle** *Child.* **Label the right circle** *Now.* **Then compare and contrast yourself as a young child and the adult you are today.**

Or, if you prefer, think of two ideas you would like to connect. Label each circle with one of the ideas. Then think about what the overlap between them might be.

Writing models start on page 181.

Writing Introductions and Conclusions

You learned from the video that a good piece of writing has a beginning, a middle, and an end. The GED essay is no exception! In an essay, the beginning, middle, and end are called the introduction, body, and conclusion.

An **introduction** tells the reader what you are writing about. It prepares the reader. A **conclusion** sums up what you have written about. It draws the writing to an end.

Organization is an important item on the GED essay scoring guide. The GED essay scorers look for an introduction and a conclusion as well as a strong body of support.

INTRODUCTION. A good way to introduce a GED essay is to restate the essay topic. Your introduction should also state the point you want to make about the topic. That is the thesis of your essay. Sometimes the introduction also includes an "attention grabber."

Look at this sample topic:

> **TOPIC**
>
> Do you think there is such a thing as harmless gossip?
>
> In your essay, explain your answer with examples from your personal knowledge, observations, and experience.

Here's a good introduction for an essay based on that topic:

> To one person, it may be harmless gossip. Yet to another, it's vicious gossip. Gossip can never be totally harmless. By its very nature, it makes people look bad or silly to others.

Notice how this writer prepares you to read his essay. You know the essay is going to be about gossip. You know the point is that gossip is always harmful to someone. You can expect to read about experiences and situations that help prove that point. Also, the first two sentences set up an interesting contrast. They make you think, don't they?

Would the following be a good way to introduce an essay on the topic?

> Gossip is talking about other people. When people gossip about someone, that person is not there.

That short paragraph does mention the topic of gossip. However, it just defines gossip. You can't tell whether the writer thinks gossip can sometimes be harmless. Also, nothing grabs your attention. You don't especially want to continue reading, do you?

CONCLUSION. A good way to write a conclusion is to restate your thesis. You should definitely not bring up any new points in your conclusion. You may, however, try to leave your reader with something to think about.

Here's a good conclusion for the essay on gossip:

> Someone is always hurt by gossip. That's why I'm careful when I talk about others. I always try to tell stories about other people the same way they would tell those stories themselves. I think that's only fair—don't you?

Notice that the introduction and conclusion do not contain much detail. The introduction prepares you for the supporting ideas in the body of the essay. The conclusion sums up the body.

GED ESSAY PRACTICE

INTRODUCTIONS AND CONCLUSIONS

A. Reread the essay topic in the box on page 76. Think briefly of your experiences with gossip. Write an introduction based on this topic. In your introduction, first restate the essay topic in your own words. Then add your thesis statement. Make sure it answers the question, *Is there such a thing as harmless gossip?*

_____

_____

_____

_____

_____

_____

B. Review the writings you have put in your portfolio so far. Choose one or two that you can add an introduction and conclusion to. Use the writing checklists below to help you.

Checklist for Introductions
- ❑ Did you state your topic clearly?
- ❑ Did you include a thesis statement that tells the main point of your writing?
- ❑ Did you include a fact, idea, or question that will get the attention of your reader?

Checklist for Conclusions
- ❑ Did you restate your thesis statement?
- ❑ Did you leave your reader with something to think about?

Feedback starts on page 181.

For more practice with introductions and conclusions, see page 151.

GED Review: Organized Writing

Here's a GED-type topic for writing an essay:

TOPIC

Is being connected to nature very important for people these days?

In your essay, explain your views, based on your personal knowledge, experiences, and observations.

Now read Antonya's essay based on this topic. As you read, pay attention to its organization. Does Antonya have an introduction and a conclusion? Are the paragraphs well organized?

Connected to Nature

(A)

As I was growing up, I spent many of my days outdoors. My brothers and I played in the woods near our house. We were far from town. We were often lonely. But at least we had a safe place to play.

(B)

When I was a teenager, my family moved to the city. I was very happy about that. I wanted to go to a big high school and walk to the drugstore to buy makeup and chewing gum anytime I wanted to.

(C)

I didn't miss those woods, not one bit. I was too old to play outside anyway.

(D)

Now I'm raising kids in the city myself. We have no yard. It's not safe for my kids to go to the park without me. They have to stay indoors too much. I wish they could be connected to nature. I think the best thing is when schools have nature programs for city kids, so that the kids get to go on field trips and learn about the environment. The park districts have good programs too sometimes. I try to take my kids to the parks in the country sometimes so they can be outdoors.

A. Review the paragraphs in Antonya's essay.

1. Read paragraph A in Antonya's essay again. Choose one:
   a. Antonya's first paragraph is a good introduction to the essay.
   b. Antonya needs a new first paragraph to introduce her essay.

2. Read paragraphs B and C in Antonya's essay again. Choose one:
   a. Paragraphs B and C read well just as they are.
   b. Paragraphs B and C should be combined into one paragraph.

GED REVIEW

3. Read paragraph D in Antonya's essay again. Choose one:
   a. Paragraph D reads well just as it is.
   b. Paragraph D should be divided into two paragraphs.

4. Choose one:
   a. Antonya should write a conclusion for her essay.
   b. Antonya's essay already has a good conclusion.

B. Complete a chart with your own responses to the essay topic.

Question: Is being connected to nature important to people these days?

REASONS TO ANSWER YES	REASONS TO ANSWER NO

Now plan how you will use these ideas in an essay of your own. You can use an outline (see page 48) if you like, or draw a picture, such as a table (see pages 46–47). You might even want to try a guiding hand, as you saw in the video.

C. Write an essay in response to the topic.

Draft and revise your essay. Practice your organization skills from this lesson.

❑ Write an introduction that restates the topic and also states your thesis. Be sure to restate the topic in your own words.

❑ Write a specific topic sentence for each paragraph.

❑ Develop one supporting idea in each paragraph. Make sure that all the details in each paragraph relate to the supporting idea.

❑ Use transitions to help your reader understand the flow of your ideas.

❑ Write a conclusion that restates your thesis and leaves your reader with something to think about.

Answers and feedback start on page 181.

Effective Sentences

LESSON GOALS

WRITING SKILLS

- Write complete sentences and correct fragments and run-ons
- Write compound sentences
- Write complex sentences

WRITER'S TOOL

- Combine sentences

GED ESSAY CONNECTION

- Use a variety of sentence types

GED REVIEW

EXTRA PRACTICE, PP. 152–155

- Complete Sentences
- Compound Sentences
- Complex Sentences
- GED Essay

1. Think About the Topic

The program you are about to watch is about writing *Effective Sentences*. This video will show you how to write a variety of sentences and how to recognize problems with sentences.

Throughout this video, you will hear teachers and professional writers discuss the importance of correct, complete sentences. One teacher discusses why such sentences are more important when you are writing than when you are speaking to someone. Why do you think that is true?

2. Prepare to Watch the Video

In this program, you will hear people talk about how the sentences you use can determine the rhythm of your writing. Try writing a piece with a quick, choppy rhythm.

_____

_____

_____

_____

You might have written something similar to this: *I left for work. I was very late. I had to drive. My car was old. It had trouble starting. It stuttered and stopped a lot. I barely made it on time.*

3. Preview the Questions

Read the questions under *Think About the Program* on the next page and keep them in mind as you watch the program. After you watch, use the questions to review the main ideas in the program.

4. Study the Vocabulary

Review the terms to the right. Understanding the meaning of writing vocabulary will help you understand the video and the rest of this lesson.

WATCH THE PROGRAM

As you watch the program, pay special attention to the host who introduces or summarizes major ideas that you need to learn about. The host will also tell you important information about the GED Writing Test.

AFTER YOU WATCH

1. Think About the Program

Why are clear and complete sentences important to your writing?

What are some of the various types of sentence structures?

Why should you vary sentence structure and length in your writing?

How can you identify fragments and run-ons?

2. Make the Connection

Think back to the woman in the video who talks about the difference between speaking and writing. In a journal or on a separate sheet of paper, write about your day. Then tell a friend or family member about your day. Notice the differences in how you write about the events of your day and how you speak about them.

comma splice— a compound sentence mistakenly written without the conjunction

complex sentence— a sentence made up of a complete thought (main clause) and an incomplete thought (dependent thought)

compound sentence— two simple sentences connected with a comma and a conjunction

conjunction—a connecting word

fragment—an incomplete sentence

predicate—the part of a sentence that tells the action or describes the subject. The predicate always includes a verb.

run-on sentence— a compound sentence mistakenly written without the comma and conjunction

sentence—a complete thought

simple sentence— a sentence with just one subject and one predicate

subject—the part of a sentence that tells who or what is acting or being described in the sentence

verb—a word that shows action or a state of being

"To write, you really have to fall in love with sentences."

Complete Thoughts

Why Are Complete Sentences Important?

A **sentence** is a complete thought. Every sentence you write should help your reader understand your message. However, a sentence can be confusing—especially if it's not really a sentence! For example, read the paragraph below. Underline any confusing "sentences" that are really incomplete thoughts.

> Taco Dan's is the best Tex-Mex cooking in town. A plateful of soft tacos. Dan serves up a great burrito with melted cheese on top. Also having a children's menu.

Did you notice any problems? You probably underlined two incomplete sentences: the second and the fourth.

Completing Fragments

An incomplete sentence is a **fragment**. It has something missing. You might remember from the program that a complete sentence has a subject and a predicate. The **subject** tells you who or what is acting or being described. The **predicate** tells you the action or describes the state of the subject. A **verb** is always part of the predicate. It is the word that shows the action (such as *take*) or the state of being (such as *is* or *seem*).

Look at what's missing from the fragments in the paragraph about Taco Dan's.

EXAMPLE

Fragment: A plateful of soft tacos.

Complete sentence: A plateful of soft tacos is enough for two people.

The predicate was missing from that fragment. You might have wondered, *What about the plateful of soft tacos? Did the writer forget something?*

EXAMPLE

Fragment: Also having a children's menu.

Complete sentence: Taco Dan's also has a children's menu.

The subject was missing from that fragment. You might have thought, *That sentence doesn't start out right.* When the writer added the subject, she had to change the verb too—from *having* to *has*.

You can learn to spot fragments in your own writing. To find fragments, use your ear. Read each sentence in your writing out loud. Does it sound complete?

When you edit, use these tips to find fragments:

- Read each sentence out loud. Does it *sound* like a complete thought?
- Check for the subject. Who or what is the sentence about?
- Check for the predicate. Does the sentence tell you something about the subject?

A. Write _C_ next to each complete sentence. Write _F_ next to each fragment.

_____ **1.** We love going out to dinner.

_____ **2.** We can all order something different.

_____ **3.** No dirty dishes.

_____ **4.** Going home with treats in doggy bags.

_____ **5.** We don't have a dog!

B. Rewrite these fragments as complete sentences. The first one is done for you.

1. Going to the stock car races.

   My friends and I are going to the stock car races.

2. Riding all night long.

   _____

3. Drivers from all over the country.

   _____

4. Tired at the end of the day.

   _____

C. Read the group of words below carefully. Decide if it is a fragment or a complete sentence. Then choose the _one best answer_ to the question.

   <u>Ready</u> for a night on the town.

   Which is the best way to write the underlined portion of this sentence? If the original is the best way, choose option (1).

   (1) Ready

   (2) Readying

   (3) Marissa is ready

   (4) Being ready

   (5) Getting ready

Answers and models start on page 182.

WRITING SKILLS

Attaching Fragments

Sometimes a fragment should be part of a nearby sentence. Here's a paragraph with two fragments like that. The fragments are in **bold**.

> Today was a tough day. I had to fire two employees. **Because I caught them stealing food from the cooler.** I called the district office and asked if I had to call the police. Nelson told me he would handle it. The officer came by here anyway. **Asking all kinds of questions about the two guys.**

Look at the first fragment—*Because I caught them stealing food from the cooler*. It has a subject and a predicate. However, it's not a complete thought. The first word, *Because*, is a clue that the thought needs more information to be complete. The meaning of the fragment depends on the information in the sentence before it. Therefore, you can fix the fragment by attaching it to that sentence:

EXAMPLE

Unattached fragment:	I had to fire two employees. Because I caught them stealing food from the cooler.
Complete sentence:	I had to fire two employees because I caught them stealing food from the cooler.

The second fragment is *Asking all kinds of questions about the two guys*. This fragment is missing a subject. However, it can be attached to the sentence that comes right before it:

EXAMPLE

Unattached fragment:	The officer came by here anyway. Asking all kinds of questions about the two guys.
Complete sentence:	The officer came by here anyway, asking all kinds of questions about the two guys.

There is never just one way to fix a fragment. For example, you could also fix the sentence fragment by adding words to complete the thought:

EXAMPLE

Separate sentences:	The officer came by here anyway. He asked all kinds of questions about the two guys.

To fix a fragment, try different ways:

Read the fragment along with the sentences before and after it. Does it seem to belong to one of those sentences?

- If so, add it to that sentence. (You might have to revise a little bit.)
- If not, add words to make the fragment a separate, complete sentence.
- Decide which version you like best.

A. Write *C* next to each pair of correct sentences. Write *F* if one of the sentences is a fragment.

_____ **I.** I had to stop by Village Hall. To register my new bicycle.

_____ **2.** While I was there. I also registered to vote.

_____ **3.** I looked at all the new job postings. And took an application form.

_____ **4.** The clerk in the personnel office was nice. I asked her out for coffee.

_____ **5.** You can get almost anything you need at Village Hall. Even a date!

B. Fix the three fragments in the following paragraph. If possible, attach each fragment to the sentence before or after it. Rewrite the paragraph on the lines below.

I am a driver for a commercial laundry. I deliver clean linens and uniforms. To hotels and restaurants on my route. I also pick up all the dirty laundry from the customers. It's hard work. When new customers meet me. They are sometimes very surprised. They expect a truck driver to be a big guy. I'm a woman, and I weigh about a hundred pounds. I like being strong. And working hard.

_____

_____

_____

_____

_____

_____

C. Read the pair of sentences below carefully. Decide if one is a fragment. Then choose the <u>one best answer</u> to the question.

If you must make a police <u>report. We ask</u> that you contact the district office first.

Which is the best way to write the underlined portion of this sentence? If the original is the best way, choose option (1).

(1) report. We ask

(2) report. Asking

(3) report. To ask

(4) report, we ask

(5) report, ask

Answers and models start on page 182.
For more practice with complete sentences, see page 152.

"It takes a certain amount of control to write a good compound sentence."

Writing Compound Sentences

What Is a Compound Sentence?

A **simple sentence** has just one subject and predicate:

subject   predicate

Pablo   fixed the leak in the kitchen.

As you heard in the program, many simple sentences together sound choppy. Good writing has a smooth rhythm. That rhythm is created by the writer. The writer creates it by using a variety of sentence structures.

One way to vary sentence structure is to put two simple sentences together. The new sentence is a **compound sentence**. (*Compound* means "more than one.")

subject   predicate   subject   predicate

Pablo   fixed the leak in the kitchen, and then he went out.

Do you remember the FANBOYS (or BOYSFAN) connecting words from the program? These **conjunctions,** along with a comma, connect simple sentences in compound sentences. The conjunctions show how the ideas in the simple sentences are related.

For And	The most common FANBOYS conjunctions are *and, but, or,* and *so.*
Nor But Or Yet So	Pablo fixed the leak, and then he went out. Pablo fixed the leak, but he didn't turn the water back on. Pablo can fix the leak, or he can call a plumber. Pablo fixed the leak, so we can use the sink now.

Look at the simple sentence *after* each conjunction in the chart above. Read each simple sentence out loud. Notice that each one is a complete sentence. Also notice the meaning of each conjunction.

To create a compound sentence:
- Write a simple sentence.
- Add a comma and then a FANBOYS conjunction.
- Add another simple sentence that is related to the idea of the first sentence.

There's another way to vary your sentences. You can use compound subjects and compound predicates. (Remember that *compound* means "more than one.")

Compound subject: subject   subject   predicate

<u>Pablo</u> and <u>Johnny</u> <u>fixed</u> the leak in the kitchen.

Compound predicate: subject   predicate   predicate

<u>Pablo</u> <u>fixed</u> the leak and <u>replaced</u> the faucet.

However, *don't* use a comma in a compound subject or compound predicate. *Do* use a comma to join a compound sentence.

EFFECTIVE SENTENCES ▪ PRACTICE 3

A. Write C next to each <u>correct compound sentence</u>.

_____ **1.** The weather turned cooler, and leaves began to fall.

_____ **2.** My sister-in-law Corinna, and Joe took Mama to the restaurant.

_____ **3.** I don't have a bike, so I have to walk.

_____ **4.** You can send that package by UPS, or mail it.

B. Create compound sentences. Insert a comma and conjunction on each line. Choose the FANBOYS conjunction that best relates the ideas in the two simple sentences.

1. Laura's wedding dress didn't fit her daughter _____
Nikki saved up for a new one.

2. I can't swim _____ I can run faster than anyone.

3. He works in the warehouse _____ she works in the front office.

4. You can pay now _____ you can pay later.

Write your own compound sentence here:

5. _____

C. Read the following sentence carefully. Decide if it is a correct compound sentence. Then choose the <u>one best answer</u> to the question.

We have money for the rent, but we can't pay the store bill.

Which correction should be made to this sentence?

(1) insert a comma after <u>money</u>

(2) remove the comma after <u>rent</u>

(3) replace <u>but</u> with <u>or</u>

(4) replace <u>but</u> with <u>so</u>

(5) no correction is necessary

Answers and models start on page 182.
For more practice with compound sentences, see page 153.

Comma Splices

Sometimes writers make a mistake with compound sentences. They leave out the conjunction. A compound sentence without a conjunction is a **comma splice**. Because you know how to write a compound sentence, you can find and correct comma splices.

EXAMPLE

> **Comma splice:** We had rehearsed for weeks, we sang perfectly.
>
> **Correct sentence:** We had rehearsed for weeks, so we sang perfectly.

Now you try it. Edit the comma splice below to make a correct compound sentence. Use a caret (∧) to insert a conjunction.

> **Comma splice:** Sally was too sick to sing, her stand-in did a great job.

Did you insert a conjunction after the comma? The best conjunction to fit with the ideas in this sentence is *but*.

To correct a comma splice:

- Make sure that you're really working with a compound sentence. Are two simple sentences joined into one sentence?
- Insert a FANBOYS conjunction after the comma. Choose a conjunction that makes sense in the sentence.

Run-on Sentences

Sometimes a writer leaves out *both* the conjunction *and* the comma in a compound sentence. This error is a **run-on sentence**. Run-on sentences are especially hard for a reader to understand.

EXAMPLE

> **Run-on sentence:** The doors were closed the stage lights went up.
>
> **Correct sentence:** The doors were closed, and the stage lights went up.

Now you try it. Edit the run-on below to make a correct compound sentence. Use a caret to insert a comma and conjunction where they belong

> **Run-on sentence:** The concert was long there was a short intermission.

Did you insert a comma and a conjunction after the word *long*? The best conjunction to fit with the ideas in this sentence is *so*. You could also use *and*.

To correct a run-on:

- Make sure that you're really working with a compound sentence. Are two simple sentences joined into one sentence?
- Put a comma and a FANBOYS conjunction after the first simple sentence.

A. Place a check mark next to each correct compound sentence. Write *CS* next to each comma splice. Write *RO* next to each run-on.

_____ **1.** I left an hour early, but I was still late for the interview.
_____ **2.** There's no bus service on Sunday night you'll have to drive me.
_____ **3.** The subway runs all night, but I don't feel safe riding alone.
_____ **4.** The nearest station is Waterston, you can take the train from there.
_____ **5.** Take a taxi from the station to my house it's too far to walk.

B. Correct the comma splices and run-ons below. Rewrite them as correct compound sentences. One sentence does not need correcting. Write *Correct* on the line.

1. Ricky paid the phone bill he forgot to pay the cable company.

_____

2. There are trees down everywhere, our electricity is out.

_____

3. We don't have a computer, yet I can get e-mail at the library.

_____

4. The gas company has a new payment plan we might try it for a year.

_____

5. The plumber cut off all the water you can't take a shower.

_____

C. Read the following sentence carefully. Decide if it is a correct compound sentence. Then choose the <u>one best answer</u> to the question.

Marina is our PR aide, she will give you a tour of the building.

Which correction should be made to this sentence?
(1) remove the comma after <u>aide</u>
(2) insert <u>and</u> after the comma
(3) remove <u>she</u>
(4) insert a comma after <u>tour</u>
(5) no correction is necessary

Answers and models start on page 182.

"A complex sentence is a really powerful strategy that a writer can use because you're indicating the relationship between two thoughts."

Writing Complex Sentences

What Is a Complex Sentence?

Look at the two parts of the following sentence. Could each part stand on its own as a complete thought?

main clause   dependent clause

We can't finish the repair today because we are missing a part.

The answer is no. The second part is not complete. That sentence is a complex sentence. A **complex sentence** is made up of a complete thought and an incomplete thought.

You might remember from the program that the incomplete thought is called a **dependent clause**. A dependent clause has its own subject and predicate. However, it *depends* on another clause to complete it.

The other clause is the **main clause**. The main clause, or independent clause, is always a complete thought by itself. In fact, the main clause could also be a simple sentence.

A dependent clause always begins with a conjunction like *because*. Here are some common conjunctions that start dependent clauses. These conjunctions help you show contrast, time, and cause-effect relationships.

Dependent Conjunctions		
Contrast	*Time*	*Cause-Effect*
although, though, unless	as, after, before, since, when, while, until	because, if, since, so that, whenever

EXAMPLES

    Contrast: You cannot enter unless you have a pass.
    Time: Things haven't been the same since you've been gone.
    Cause-effect: I can go tomorrow if I clean the house today.

In a complex sentence, the dependent clause can come before or after the main clause. Here is the same sentence with *because* as above. However, the order of the clauses is reversed. Do you notice anything else that's different? Look at the punctuation.

dependent clause   main clause

Because we are missing a part, we can't finish the repair today.

When a dependent clause begins the sentence, place a comma after it.

A. Place a check mark next to each correct complex sentence.

_____ 1. I kept the radio on because a big storm was coming.

_____ 2. While the baby slept peacefully, the storm raged.

_____ 3. I should have gone to the basement, but I didn't want to wake the baby.

_____ 4. I foolishly sat by the window to watch the storm.

_____ 5. Although we were safe, many homes were damaged by a tornado.

B. Complete each complex sentence below. Choose a dependent conjunction that fits the meaning of the sentence. Write it on the line. Add a comma after a dependent clause that begins a sentence. The first sentence is done for you.

1. _____When_____ the sun came up, we saw standing water everywhere.

2. _____ the storm had been terrible it was a gorgeous morning.

3. Some friends called for help_____their roof was torn off.

4. _____TV crews roamed the trailer park residents stared at their ruined homes.

5. Many families will live in local hotels _____ their homes are repaired.

Write a complex sentence of your own. Put the dependent clause at the end.

6. _____.

Now change the order of the clauses. Put the dependent clause at the beginning.

7. _____.

C. Read the following sentence carefully. Decide if it is a correct complex sentence. Then choose the one best answer to the question.

Many workers were affected by the storm, we will operate the plant on short shifts today.

Which correction should be made to this sentence?

(1) replace <u>Many</u> with <u>Because many</u>

(2) replace <u>Many</u> with <u>Although many</u>

(3) remove the comma after <u>storm</u>

(4) insert <u>but</u> before <u>we</u>

(5) no correction is necessary

Answers and models start on page 182.
For more practice with complex sentences, see page 154.

Combining Sentences

When you read your writing, you may find too many short choppy sentences. To revise, you can combine some sentences. Two sentences can be combined to make one complex sentence:

EXAMPLES

Simple sentences:	New employees have four days of training. Then they are paired with experienced workers.
Complex sentence:	After new employees have four days of training, they are paired with experienced workers.

Two sentences can also be combined to make one compound sentence:

Compound sentence:	New employees have four days of training, and then they are paired with experienced workers.

Which Should You Write?

Complex and compound sentences help your reader understand your meaning. Together with simple sentences, they also help create a rhythm to your writing.

Often you have more than one good way to write an idea. See the different ways these three simple sentences can be rewritten. Notice there are some differences in meaning. The meaning can change depending on the conjunction and the sentence structure:

Simple sentences:	The new employees will start on Monday. They won't work shifts until Friday. They will be evaluated the following week.

Although the new employees will start on Monday, they won't work shifts until Friday. They will be evaluated the following week.

The new employees will start on Monday, but they won't work shifts until Friday. They will be evaluated the following week.

The new employees will start on Monday. Because they won't work shifts until Friday, they will be evaluated the following week.

The new employees will start on Monday. They won't work shifts until Friday, so they will be evaluated the following week.

To choose a way to write or revise an idea, ask yourself:

- Which way best gets my meaning across to my reader?
- Which way sounds best with the sentences around it?

A. Circle the letter of the revision that has the clearest meaning for a reader.

1. New workers must fill out forms. Then they can be paid.
   a. New workers must fill out forms, and they can be paid.
   b. New workers must fill out forms before they can be paid.

2. Perhaps you are not a U.S. citizen. Then you must show a green card.
   a. If you are not a U.S. citizen, you must show a green card.
   b. Perhaps you are not a U.S. citizen, but you must show a green card.

B. Combine each pair of sentences into a complex sentence. It's OK to change some of the words. Use the chart of dependent conjunctions on page 90 if you need to.

1. Get to know people on your shift. You will be able to ask them questions.

   _____

2. Martin will join your shift on Friday. He will have finished his training.

   _____

Combine each pair of sentences into a compound sentence. Use a comma and a FANBOYS conjunction.

3. Nadia is an expert operator. She trains people to use the grinder.

   _____

4. You must follow the safety rules. You could get hurt.

   _____

C. Read the following sentence carefully. Decide which revision is best. Then choose the <u>one best answer</u> to the question.

The new workers will learn <u>quickly. They</u> are a smart group.

Which is the best way to write the underlined portion of these sentences? If the original is the best way, choose option (1).

(1) quickly. They
(2) quickly, and they
(3) quickly since they
(4) quickly unless they
(5) quickly, so they

Answers and models start on page 182.

Combining Sentences

Writers often spend time tinkering with their sentences. They enjoy trying new ways of putting their ideas together. Sentence combining helps them do that.

Sentence combining helps writing flow more smoothly. Combining sentences also helps get rid of repeated words and ideas.

Use an Opening Phrase

The sentences below have the same subject. The combined revision gets rid of the repeated subject. The new sentence also has an opening phrase.

EXAMPLE

> **Repetition:** <u>We</u> went to the art museum. <u>We</u> saw paintings and sculpture.
> **Opening phrase:** At the art museum, we saw paintings and sculpture.

Punctuation rule: Put a comma after an opening phrase.

Use an Ending Phrase

In this example, two sentences do not have exactly the same subject. However, the subjects refer to the same person. In the combined revision, the writer uses an ending phrase.

EXAMPLE

> **Repetition:** <u>Lee</u> ran away from the fire. <u>He</u> grabbed his son by the hand.
> **Ending phrase:** Lee ran away from the fire, grabbing his son by the hand.

Punctuation rule: If an ending phrase begins with an *-ing* verb, like the one above, you usually need a comma before it.

Use a Renaming Phrase

In this example, the first sentence introduces someone, and the next sentence explains who he is. In the combined revision, a renaming phrase replaces the second sentence.

EXAMPLE

> **Repetition:** I met <u>Joshua</u> at the radio station. <u>Joshua</u> is Tara's brother.
> **Renaming phrase:** I met Joshua, Tara's brother, at the radio station.

Punctuation rule: Use commas to set off a renaming phrase if the phrase isn't necessary to know who is being named.

USING THE WRITER'S TOOL ■ COMBINE SENTENCES

WRITER'S TOOL

A. Combine the following pairs of sentences by using an opening phrase. Don't forget the comma. The first one is done for you.

1. We were on our way to the airport. We asked Larry if he had the tickets.
   On our way to the airport, we asked Larry if he had the tickets.

2. We were on the plane at last. We breathed a sigh of relief.

3. We walked down the ramp. We could see his folks waving at us.

B. Combine the following pairs of sentences by using an ending phrase. Use an *-ing* verb to start your ending phrase. Don't forget the comma.

1. I think it's wonderful being a tourist. I can explore a new place all day long.

2. Moe loves to walk through strange cities. He looks at the people and the buildings.

3. Laurel visits art museums. She drinks in paintings with her eyes.

C. Combine the following pairs of sentences by using a renaming phrase. Don't forget to use commas.

1. Laurel has taken many art classes. She is a painter.

2. Laurel helped Rafael learn to paint landscapes. Rafael is her best student.

 D. Review your writings. Try to combine some sentences of your own!

Writing models begin on page 183.

Vary Your Sentences

Nobody wants to be monotonous. *Monotonous* means same, dull, flat, boring. In the program and in this lesson, you have learned about writing with rhythm. Good writing never sounds monotonous. Instead, it dances a little—as if to a beat.

Putting a little dance into your essay will help you score high on the GED Test. You can do that by varying your sentences.

Keep in mind, though, that you can't *read* sentence rhythm. You have to *hear* it! To hear the rhythm of your writing, read it out loud. If it sounds monotonous, work on your sentences. Combine them; change them; even break them up.

Short Sentences

Short sentences have impact. They make the point. They stop you in your tracks.

> What's that? Watch out!

Get the idea? Try short sentences.

Long Sentences

Long sentences are graceful, thoughtful. They give the reader time to think through an idea along with you. Long sentences help readers take time to absorb an idea or picture a scene. At the same time, they help the writer pack in details.

> When you create a long, flowing sentence, you carry the reader along on an easy stream of words.

Get the idea?

Revising for Sentence Variety

To revise your own writing, start by reading it out loud. Listen for sentences that sound flat, dull, monotonous. For example, read these flat-sounding sentences out loud:

> This book is very good. Every chapter is a new story. The stories are about different careers. I'm learning a lot from reading it.

If you find a passage like that in your writing, play around with it. Exercise your sentence muscles on it. Make a complex sentence, a compound sentence, a short sentence, a long sentence. Create a question. Add opening, closing, or renaming phrases to your sentences.

Here's a revision of the passage with varied sentences. Read it out loud. Use expression and emphasis so that you can hear the rhythm. Notice how different it is from the first version!

Need a good book about careers? In this book, every chapter tells a story about a different career. I'm learning a lot from reading it.

GED ESSAY PRACTICE

VARY YOUR SENTENCES

A. On a separate sheet of paper, revise each group of sentences to vary the rhythm and length. See how many different types of sentences and phrases you can use!

1. Kyle hurt his ankle at the softball game. He couldn't stand on it. We took him to the emergency room.

2. Kyle had an X ray taken. The X ray showed a broken ankle. The doctor gave him a splint. The doctor was an orthopedist.

3. Kyle can take the splint on and off. It has Velcro straps. He takes it off to shower.

 B. Review the writings in your portfolio. Choose a paragraph or essay. Revise it to improve the variety of your sentences. Follow this plan:

❑ Read your writing out loud. Underline any sentences that repeat or sound monotonous.

❑ Combine sentences to get rid of repeated words and ideas.

❑ Create at least one short sentence that makes a strong impact.

❑ Create at least one long, flowing sentence.

C. Write about the following topic. Use the skills you have learned in this book. Review the Writing Process and checklists in the Handbook on pages 190–191. As you revise your writing, work on your sentences. Combine ideas. Try out long and short sentences for different effects.

TOPIC

Some people view work as a way to pay the bills. Other people view work as a way to develop themselves.

What is your view of work? Write an essay explaining what work has meant in your life.

Answers and models start on page 183.
For more practice with varying sentence structure, see page 155.

GED Review: Effective Sentences

Choose the one best answer to each question.

Questions 1 through 4 refer to the following letter to a customer.

Dear Dan:

(A)

(1) Thank you for your call this morning. (2) I certainly understand why you were upset, I am very sorry that we printed your menus on the wrong color paper.

(B)

(3) Because you are a valued customer at Speedy Printing. (4) We would like to make this up to you. (5) We have reprinted your menus on the correct paper and I would also like to offer you a special discount for the next three months. (6) Your orders at a 20 percent discount through July 1.

(C)

(7) I hope you'll be bringing us your business for many years to come, Dan. (8) Best of luck with the new menu.

Sincerely,
Alicia Rodales, President

1. Sentence 2: **I certainly understand why you were upset, I am very sorry that we printed your menus on the wrong color paper.**

   Which correction should be made to sentence 2?
   (1) insert a comma after <u>understand</u>
   (2) change the comma to a question mark
   (3) insert <u>and</u> after the comma
   (4) insert a comma after <u>sorry</u>
   (5) no correction is necessary

2. Sentences 3 and 4: **Because you are a valued customer at Speedy <u>Printing</u>. <u>We</u> would like to make this up to you.**

   Which is the best way to write the underlined portion of these sentences? If the original is the best way, choose option (1).
   (1) Printing. We
   (2) Printing, we
   (3) Printing, but we
   (4) Printing we
   (5) Printing and we

3. Sentence 5: **We have reprinted your menus on the correct paper and I would also like to offer you a special discount for the next three months.**

   Which correction should be made to sentence 5?
   (1) insert a comma after <u>paper</u>
   (2) remove <u>and</u> before <u>I</u>
   (3) replace <u>I would also like</u> with <u>liking</u>
   (4) insert a comma after <u>discount</u>
   (5) no correction is necessary

4. Sentence 6: **<u>Your orders</u> at a 20 percent discount through July 1.**

   Which is the best way to write the underlined portion of this sentence? If the original is the best way, choose option (1).
   (1) Your orders
   (2) For you, orders
   (3) Giving your orders
   (4) Your ordering
   (5) You can order

Questions 5 through 8 refer to the following article.

Writing Business Letters: Think of the Audience!

(A)

(1) Are you familiar with writing business letters? (2) When you write a business letter you must always think of your audience. (3) People are busy when they are at work, you can make it easy for them to read your letter.

(B)

(4) Business letters should always get right to the point. (5) State the purpose of your letter right in the first paragraph. (6) In the body of your letter, explain the most important details. (7) If you need to send a lot of information, put the rest of the details on a separate page.

(C)

(8) A clean letter is easier to read than a messy one. (9) So be as neat as you can. (10) Proofread for any mistakes. (11) Your letter will make a good impression!

5. Sentence 2: **When you write a business letter you must always think of your audience.**

   Which correction should be made to sentence 2?
   (1) replace <u>When</u> with <u>Because</u>
   (2) replace <u>When you write</u> with <u>When writing</u>
   (3) insert a comma after <u>letter</u>
   (4) insert <u>and</u> after <u>letter</u>
   (5) insert a comma after <u>always</u>

6. Sentence 3: **People are busy when they are at <u>work, you</u> can make it easy for them to read your letter.**

   Which is the best way to write the underlined portion of this sentence? If the original is the best way, choose option (1).
   (1) work, you
   (2) work you
   (3) work for you
   (4) work, but you
   (5) work, or you

7. Sentence 7: **If you need to send a lot of information, put the rest of the details on a separate page.**

   Which correction should be made to sentence 7?
   (1) replace <u>If you need</u> with <u>Needing</u>
   (2) replace <u>If</u> with <u>Because</u>
   (3) remove the comma after <u>information</u>
   (4) insert <u>so</u> after the comma
   (5) no correction is necessary

8. Sentences 8 and 9: **A clean letter is easier to read than a messy <u>one. So</u> be as neat as you can.**

   Which is the best way to write the underlined portion of these sentences? If the original is the best way, choose option (1).
   (1) one. So
   (2) one so
   (3) one, so
   (4) one, and
   (5) one, but

Answers and explanations start on page 183.

Grammar and Usage

LESSON GOALS

WRITING SKILLS

- Use nouns and the correct pronoun form
- Use the correct verb form and tense
- Make sure subjects and verbs agree

WRITER'S TOOL

- Peer edit

GED ESSAY CONNECTION

- Choose your words

GED REVIEW

EXTRA PRACTICE, PP. 156–159

- Nouns and Pronouns
- Verb Tense
- Subject-Verb Agreement
- GED Essay

1. Think About the Topic

You are about to watch a program on *Grammar and Usage*. This video will help you understand some of the basic rules of English grammar.

In the program, writing teachers and professional writers discuss how correct grammar is important to good writing. They will talk about how your writing can represent you, either positively or negatively. One woman compares how you write to how you dress. How could what you write influence what others think of you?

2. Prepare to Watch the Video

In this program, you will learn that verbs give readers a sense of time. You will see how the particular verb tense you use lets your reader know when the events you are talking about took place. Write a brief paragraph describing what you did yesterday morning; remember to use verbs in the past tense.

_____

_____

_____

_____

You may have written something like this: *I woke up at 7:30. I ate breakfast, and drove to the post office. I bought some stamps, mailed a letter, and then went to work.*

3. Preview the Questions

Read the questions under *Think About the Program* on the next page and keep them in mind as you watch the program. After you watch, use the questions to review the main ideas in the program.

4. Study the Vocabulary

Review the terms to the right. Understanding the meaning of writing vocabulary will help you understand the video and the rest of the lesson.

WATCH THE PROGRAM

As you watch the program, pay special attention to the host who introduces or summarizes major ideas that you need to learn about. The host will also tell you important information about the GED Writing Test.

AFTER YOU WATCH

1. Think About the Program

Why is it important to use proper grammar when writing?

How can the message, or point, of your piece be affected by your grammar?

How can reading aloud help you correct your writing?

Is it necessary to know all the rules of grammar?

2. Make the Connection

Throughout the video, people explain how mistakes in grammar can take a reader's attention away from the meaning of a piece of writing. Read newspapers and magazines to see if you can find any grammatical errors. How do they affect the message the author is trying to get across?

antecedent—the noun to which a pronoun refers in a sentence

compound subject—a subject that has more than one noun joined by a conjunction

irregular verb—a verb that does not follow the regular pattern of present-tense and past-tense forms

noun—a word that names a person, place, thing, or idea

peer editing—the practice of exchanging your writing with a friend or classmate and making comments and suggestions on each other's work

pronoun—a word that takes the place of a noun in a sentence

verb—the part of a sentence that tells the subject's action (for example, *run, sing, break*) or helps tell the subject's state or condition (for example, *is, appear, seem*)

verb tense—the time (past, present, future) when the action of a verb takes place

"A lot of people have trouble deciding which pronouns to use. To help keep this straight, remember that the pronoun form depends on the noun it replaces."

Nouns and Pronouns

People, Places, Things, Ideas

Do you remember the teacher in the video writing *chair, Steve,* and *freedom* on the board? Each of those words is a noun. A **noun** names a person, a place, a thing, or an idea. Nouns are one of the basic building blocks of sentences.

Can you find the nouns in the sentences below? Underline every noun you find.

> This memo serves as a reminder that all time cards must be returned to the office on Friday. Otherwise, a warning will be issued. Forgetfulness is no excuse!

The nouns are *memo, reminder, time cards, office, Friday, warning, forgetfulness,* and *excuse.* Did you find them all?

You may have noticed that some nouns name just one thing—for example, *memo* or *excuse.* These nouns are **singular.** Other nouns name more than one thing—for example, *time cards.* A noun that names more than one thing is **plural.**

Pronouns Are Noun Substitutes

Look at the boxed words in the sentence below.

> Please return the |coat| to the rack if you don't want to buy |it|.

Both words refer to a thing, but *it* is not a noun. It's a pronoun. A **pronoun** is a word that takes the place of a noun in a sentence. In the sentence above, the pronoun *it* acts as a substitute for the noun *coat: if you don't want to buy <u>the coat.</u>*

Notice how pronouns are used to take the place of nouns below.

> The salesperson put the shirts away. She hung them on the sale rack.

In the sentences above, the pronoun *She* replaces the noun *salesperson.* The noun that a pronoun replaces is called its **antecedent.** Therefore, *salesperson* is the antecedent of *She.* What is the antecedent of *them* in the sentences above? You are correct if you said *shirts.*

The chart below shows some common pronouns. Like nouns, pronouns can be singular or plural. Think about how you use these pronouns to substitute for nouns when speaking or writing.

Singular Pronouns	Plural Pronouns
I, you, he, she, it	we, you, they
me, him, her	us, them
my, mine, your, yours, his, her, hers, its	our, ours, your, yours, their, theirs

A. **Underline the pronouns in the sentences below. Then draw an arrow connecting each pronoun to its antecedent.**

E X A M P L E :

The aunt brought gifts for the boy. He loved them.

1. Mr. Santiago saw the movie yesterday, and he enjoyed it.

2. Mr. Santiago's sons recommended the movie. His wife could not go.

3. A kind woman offered a man an aisle seat because she saw he needed help.

4. When Mr. Santiago asked some teenagers to be quiet, they stopped talking.

B. **Write sentences using the pronouns given.**

1. my _____

2. them _____

3. we _____

C. **Read the sentence below and decide if the underlined pronoun is correct. Then choose the one best answer to the question.**

I returned the pants today because <u>it</u> didn't fit right.

Which is the best way to write the underlined portion of this sentence? If the original is the best way, choose option (1).

(1) it
(2) them
(3) they
(4) their
(5) ours

Answers and explanations start on page 183.

WRITING SKILLS

Choosing the Correct Pronoun

To decide which pronoun is correct, try using your ears. Ask yourself what sounds right. As one writer in the video said, when you read an error in your writing, "It will go clunk in your head." However, it also helps to know the kinds of pronouns and how each kind can be used.

For example, some pronouns are **subject pronouns**. They can be used as the subject of a sentence. In this example, *I* is the subject:

> I will finish the filing by the end of the week.

Other pronouns are **object pronouns**. They are used as a "receiver," or as an object at the end of an action. In this example, the pronoun *me* is the object of the verb *told:*

> My boss told me to take extra time on the project.

Object pronouns are also used after prepositions, such as *between, to,* and *from,* as you saw in the video:

> Take it from me—that job is hard!

Subject pronouns are used only as subjects, and object pronouns are used only as objects. That is true even if they are paired with another subject or object:

> **Subject:** Mariah and I will finish the filing by the end of the week.
> **Object:** My boss told Mariah and me to take extra time on the project.
> **Object:** Just between you and me—that job is hard!

Still other pronouns are **possessive pronouns**. They show ownership:

> There are five hours of overtime on my paycheck.
> Mariah got four hours of overtime on hers.

The chart below shows you the kinds of pronouns and how to use them.

Subject Pronouns		Object Pronouns		Possessive Pronouns	
Singular	**Plural**	**Singular**	**Plural**	**Singular**	**Plural**
I	we	me	us	my, mine	our, ours
you	you	you	you	your, yours	your, yours
he she it	they	him her it	them	his her, hers its	their, theirs

To choose the correct pronoun, look at the noun it replaces and at the way the pronoun is used in the sentence:

- Is the noun singular or plural?
- Is the noun male, female, or neither?
- Is the pronoun used as a subject or an object, or does it show possession?

In which of these sentences are pronouns used correctly?

> The employee awards were given to her and me.
> Her and me were proud to receive the awards.
> We took her and me awards home.

The first sentence is correct. Both *her* and *me* are object pronouns. In the first sentence, they are used as the objects of the preposition *to*.

GRAMMAR AND USAGE ▪ PRACTICE 2

A. Write C above each correct pronoun. Write I above each incorrect one.

1. When you come to the beach, please bring towels for Jeff and I.

2. They can't come until later, but us will manage without them.

3. Will our plans change if Sara and him can't come?

B. Replace the underlined nouns with the correct pronouns.

_____ 1. Many people bought tickets to <u>Tom and Victor's</u> concert.

_____ 2. Tickets cost $35, but proceeds from <u>tickets</u> will go to charity.

_____ 3. <u>Tom's girlfriend</u> has not decided what to wear.

C. Read the sentence below and decide if the pronouns used are correct. Then choose the <u>one best answer</u> to the question.

> Him and I were exhausted when we got home.

Which correction should be made to this sentence?

(1) replace <u>Him</u> with <u>His</u>
(2) replace <u>Him</u> with <u>He</u>
(3) replace <u>I</u> with <u>me</u>
(4) replace <u>we</u> with <u>us</u>
(5) no correction is necessary

Answers and explanations start on page 183.
For more practice with nouns and pronouns, see page 156.

"Verbs are really essential parts of sentences. They convey a lot of information in a single word."

Verbs

What Verbs Do

A **verb** is the part of a sentence that tells what the subject of the sentence *does* or helps tell what its state or condition *is*.

- An **action verb** can show physical action (such as *run*) or mental action (such as *think*).
- A **linking verb** links the subject with a word that describes its state of being.

Physical action: A telemarketer called yesterday.
Mental action: I wanted to hang up on her.
State of being: She was pushy.

Verbs Tell Time: Present, Past, and Future

As you know from the video, verbs tell more than *what* the subject does or is. They also tell *when* the action or state of being takes place. The time that a verb tells is its **tense**.

A **present-tense** verb shows action or being that takes place now or regularly.

Even at the zoo, the lions look fierce. They pace back and forth.

Look at the verbs below. Both are in the present tense. How are they different?

A turtle moves slowly, while cheetahs move quite swiftly.

The present-tense verb form depends on the subject of the sentence. When the subject is a singular noun (like *turtle*) or the pronoun *he, she,* or *it,* the present tense form usually ends in *-s*.

A **past-tense** verb shows action that happened before. The past tense is usually formed by adding *-d* or *-ed*.

The angry baboon leaped at the crowd on the other side of the window.

A **future-tense** verb shows action that will happen at some later point. The future tense is formed by placing the **helping verb** *will* in front of the present form:

The elephant will deliver her baby in three months.

Often a clue word or phrase will tell you what tense to use in a sentence.

Look for clue words that answer the question *when* in these sentences. They will help tell you the tense of the verb.

> The package finally arrived last Monday.
> The post office usually delivers mail more efficiently than that.
> We will open the package tomorrow at the party.

First sentence: The clue *last Monday* tells you that the past tense *arrived* is needed.

Second sentence: The clue *usually* tells you that the present tense *delivers* is needed.

Third sentence: The clue *tomorrow* tells you that the future tense *will open* is needed.

GRAMMAR AND USAGE ▪ PRACTICE 3

A. Underline the verb in each sentence below. Then on the line provided, write the tense of the verb: past, present, or future.

_____ **1.** The homeless man appeared at the shelter door last night.

_____ **2.** The shelter always plans healthful meals for at least fifty guests.

_____ **3.** Ernest lived at the shelter for several months.

_____ **4.** Next week a doctor from town will provide free medical service.

B. Complete each sentence. Write the correct form and tense of the verb in parentheses.

1. Mario (own) _____ a prize-winning dog whose name is Slick.

2. Mario (raise) _____ Slick from the time he was a puppy.

3. Slick (appear) _____ next month at the dog show.

4. Mario (hope) _____ to win his third blue ribbon with Slick.

C. Read the sentence below and decide if the verb used is correct. Then choose the <u>one best answer</u> to the question.

> Tomorrow the workers <u>had</u> the day off.

Which is the best way to write the underlined portion of this sentence? If the original is the best way, choose option (1).

(1) had

(2) will have

(3) having

(4) has

(5) are

Answers and explanations start on page 184.
For more practice with verb tense, see page 157

Verb Forms

Each verb has four main parts, or forms. For example, here are the four forms of *laugh*:

Present	Past	Past Participle	Present Participle
laugh	laughed	laughed	laughing

The first two verb forms are used to create the three simple tenses you just read about:

> **Present:** I laugh whenever I see him.
> **Past:** I laughed when I saw him yesterday.
> **Future:** I will laugh when I see him tomorrow.

However, life does not happen in just those three simple tenses. You can use the other forms to create other tenses. For example, use the past participle to show an action that began in the past. Use a helping verb like *has, have,* or *had* with the past participle:

> I have laughed at his jokes for years.

Use the present participle to show a continuing action:

> I am laughing right this minute.
> I was laughing when I hurt myself.

Irregular Verbs

Most verbs form the past and past participle by adding *-ed* or *-d*. However, there is a group of verbs that do not follow this regular pattern. Not surprisingly, these verbs are called **irregular verbs**.

One way to learn irregular verb forms is to listen to correct speech. Another way is to study the verbs that give you problems. Here's a chart of common irregular verbs.

Present	Past	Past Principle	
am, is, are (forms of *be*)	was, were	been	
do, does	did	done	
has, have	had	had	
bring	brought	brought	
buy	bought	bought	
come	came	come	
go	went	gone	
run	ran	run	
see	saw	seen	
send	sent	sent	
wear	wore	worn	
begin	began	begun	These verb
drink	drank	drunk	forms have
sing	sang	sung	an *i-a-u* pattern.
swim	swam	swum	

Present	Past	Past Participle	
break	broke	broken	The past
choose	chose	chosen	participles of
fall	fell	fallen	these verbs
get	got	gotten	end with *n*.
give	gave	given	
know	knew	known	
take	took	taken	
write	wrote	written	

GRAMMAR AND USAGE ▪ PRACTICE 4

A. **Write C above each verb used correctly. Write I above each incorrect verb.**

1. TV shows been too boring or silly for too long.

2. Talented people wrote and maked TV shows years ago.

3. Last night I seen a really dull show.

4. I got so bored that I fell asleep.

B. **Write the correct form of the verb in parentheses to complete each sentence below.**

1. Yesterday an accident (take) _____ place right outside my home.

2. One car (run) _____ a red light and slammed into a woman in another car.

3. The poor woman (break) _____ her jaw and (get) _____ whiplash.

4. I have (see) _____ a lot in my life, but nothing as upsetting as that.

C. **Read the sentence below and decide if the verb used is correct. Then choose the <u>one best answer</u> to the question.**

Last month the managers <u>sended</u> out a notice that the warehouse would close.

Which is the best way to write the underlined portion of this sentence? If the original is the best way, choose option (1).

(1) sended
(2) will send
(3) send
(4) sent
(5) sends

Answers and explanations start on page 184.

WRITING SKILLS

> *"The basic rule is that a singular subject takes a singular verb. A plural subject takes a plural verb. The problem is, it's not always easy to tell if the subject is singular or plural."*

Subject-Verb Agreement

Simple Subjects

You know that the present-tense form of a verb can be used with all subjects except *he, she, it,* and singular nouns. For these exceptions, add an *-s* or *-es* to the verb:

Plural: The Carsons **watch** a movie together every Saturday night.
Singular: Most evenings I **watch** with them.
Singular: Their son **watches** only if he does not have a softball game.

Some subjects name a group of individuals—for example, *crew, jury, class, team.* However, that does not mean the subject is plural. If the individuals in the group are acting as one, the subject is singular:

Singular: The family **watches** a movie together every Saturday night.

Compound Subjects

A sentence may have a subject with more than one noun or pronoun. Then it contains a **compound subject:**

The client and her manager **want** to schedule a meeting.
Either Megan or Felipe **wants** to meet with them.

Both of those sentences have compound subjects. Then why does the first use the plural form *want* while the second uses the singular *-s* form *wants?* Here are two rules that explain why:

- When two nouns or pronouns in the subject are joined by *and*, the subject is <u>always plural</u>:

  The father and his sons **race** cars on the weekend.
  The sons and their father **race** cars on the weekend.

- When two nouns or pronouns in the subject are joined by *or* or *nor*, the verb should agree with the subject noun or pronoun <u>closest</u> to it:

  Either the father or his <u>sons</u> **own** that race car.

  plural noun—no *-s* on verb

  Either the sons or their <u>father</u> **owns** that race car.

  singular noun—use *-s* verb form

Which verb agrees with the subject in each sentence below?

Both the neighbors and Mrs. Ramirez (*thinks, think*) we should leave.
Either David or I (*read, reads*) to our son every night before bed.

You are correct if you chose *think* in the first sentence and *read* in the second sentence.

GRAMMAR AND USAGE ▪ PRACTICE 5

A. Underline the subject in each sentence below. Then write *A* above the verb if it agrees with the subject. Write *NA* if it does not agree.

1. My cousin and her brother attends the same GED class.

2. They like their teacher very much.

3. My class are studying pre-GED writing right now.

4. Either my mother or my mother-in-law sit with my toddler during school hours.

5. My child and school make life busy for me.

B. Underline the verb that agrees with the subject in each sentence below.

1. A salad and a skim milk (makes, make) up Betty's standard lunch.

2. A healthy diet and exercise (help, helps) create a healthy body.

3. Neither Betty nor her children (eat, eats) sugar after two in the afternoon.

4. Neither the kids nor Betty (is, are) overweight.

5. Skin and hair (improves, improve) with a vitamin-rich diet.

6. A long, healthy life (seem, seems) possible for more people every year.

C. Read the sentence below and decide if the subject and verb agree. Then choose the <u>one best answer</u> to the question.

When either the overnight packages or the regular mail arrive, the clerk starts sorting right away.

Which correction should be made to this sentence?
(1) change <u>arrive</u> to <u>arrived</u>
(2) change <u>arrive</u> to <u>arrives</u>
(3) change <u>starts</u> to <u>start</u>
(4) change <u>starts</u> to <u>started</u>
(5) no correction is necessary

Answers and explanations start on page 184.

Interrupters: When Words Come Between

In some sentences, it's not easy to tell if the subject is singular or plural. In other sentences, it's not easy to tell what the subject even is! That problem can happen when words come between the subject and the verb. Look at this example:

The ⬚clock⬚ hanging over the shelves ⬚is⬚ five minutes slow.

Shelves is the noun closest to the verb. You might think that the verb should be *are* to agree with the plural *shelves*. However, the actual subject of the sentence is *clock*—the clock is five minutes slow, not the shelves! The phrase *hanging over the shelves* is an interrupter. It comes between the subject and the verb.

Which verb in parentheses is correct in the sentence below? First look for the noun that is the actual subject of the sentence. Ask yourself, *Who or what is appearing?*

The police officers nearest the accident scene (*appears, appear*) almost immediately.

The subject of the sentence is plural—*police officers*. Therefore, the verb form *appear* is the correct choice. *Nearest the accident scene* is an interrupter.

Inverted Order: When Subject and Verb Are Switched

Sometimes the subject of the sentence actually follows the verb instead of coming before it. In this example, the subject *calculator* comes after the verb *is*.

Under that pile of papers ⬚is⬚ your ⬚calculator.⬚

To help find the subject, rearrange the sentence like this:

Your ⬚calculator is⬚ under that pile of papers.

The subject of both sentences is *calculator,* not *pile* nor *papers.*

Which verb should be used in this sentence? First rearrange the words in your head to find the subject.

Where (*does, do*) the file folders get stored?

If you change the order of the words, you get *The file folders do get stored where?* The subject is the plural *folders*. Therefore, the verb should be *do*.

People often start a sentence with *there* or *here*. However, those words are not nouns or pronouns. They can't be the subject of the sentence. In such sentences, the subject will come after the verb:

There ⬚are⬚ many ⬚problems⬚ with the quality of the work.
NOT There is many problems. . . . NOR There's many problems. . . .

Here <u>are</u> some <u>ways</u> to solve those problems.
NOT Here is some ways.... NOR Here's some ways....

A. Underline the subject in each sentence below. Then write _A_ above the verb if it agrees with the subject. Write _NA_ if it does not agree.

1. Before the service is usually many volunteer announcements.

2. Many people from the town help with community work.

3. Here comes all the volunteers to clean the park.

4. There is little time to help with many fund-raising events.

5. Where is the donations we need for the food pantry?

B. Underline the verb that agrees with the subject in each sentence below.

1. The members of my family (feels, feel) lucky to know a good electrician.

2. Rob Brown, who owns Brown Electric, (is, are) my uncle.

3. When the power in our rooms (go, goes) out, we call Rob.

4. There (is, are) many good reasons to leave electrical wires to the experts.

5. In the corner of that room (is, are) the circuit box.

C. Read the sentence below and decide if the subjects and verbs agree. Then choose the <u>one best answer</u> to the question.

The drivers from Easy-Transport Company become licensed for long-distance trips after their supervisor from short-distance trips sign off.

Which correction should be made to this sentence?

(1) change <u>become</u> to <u>becomes</u>
(2) change <u>become</u> to <u>became</u>
(3) change <u>sign</u> to <u>signs</u>
(4) change <u>sign</u> to <u>signing</u>
(5) no correction is necessary

Answers and explanations start on page 184.
For more practice with subject-verb agreement, see page 158.

WRITER'S TOOL

Peer Editing

You've learned how to edit your own writing as part of the writing process. However, do you think it's easy to edit your writing? Don't be afraid to say no. Many writers find self-editing difficult.

Why? Because when you are the creator of the words and ideas, you already know what you're trying to say. When you edit, it's easy to read what you mean rather than what your writing actually says!

Also, suppose a writer has problems using pronouns or verbs correctly. Chances are, that writer will have problems editing pronoun or verb errors.

Writers have a great way to solve this problem: **peer editing**. A peer editor reads your writing and gives you ideas on how to improve it. In return, you do the same for his or her writing. A peer editor can be a classmate, a friend, a coworker, a relative—anyone like you who writes.

Peer editing is a method to improve writing. Two peers read each other's writing and give feedback.

Peer-Editing Guidelines

When you have chosen someone for peer editing, exchange papers. Then follow these guidelines to read that person's work:

- **Ask the writer if you should focus on anything in particular.** Some writers have difficulty giving enough details. Other writers use sentence fragments. If you know the skills that a writer is working on, you can look for them when you read.
- **Be positive.** Before pointing out errors, find things you like about the writing and share them.
- **Look at the big picture first**. Ask yourself, *What is the main idea the writer is expressing? Are the ideas organized? What do I think of the piece as a whole?*
- **Be specific in your comments.** For example, don't just say, "I like the way you said things." Instead, circle specific words and phrases that sound good to you. If you get confused, try to point out exactly where things went wrong.

- **Make suggestions to improve the writing.** Don't just say, "This needs fixing." Try to suggest how to fix it.
- **Point out errors in grammar and usage, spelling, and punctuation.**
- **Be considerate of feelings, but don't apologize for your opinion.** Feedback is best when it is honest and meant to help, not to criticize.

USING THE WRITER'S TOOL ▪ PEER EDIT

 Choose a writing assignment from your portfolio. Ask a partner to exchange papers with you for peer editing. Use the guidelines above and the form below to get and give feedback. You may want to use a separate sheet of paper.

Peer Editing Feedback

Date: _____

Writer: _____

Peer Editor: _____

1. What are two things you like about this writing?

    _____

    _____

2. Is the writing well organized and easy to follow? Explain your view.

    _____

3. Is the word choice interesting and varied? _____

4. Are the sentences correct and well constructed?_____

5. Does the writer use correct grammar and spelling? _____

6. What are one or two things you think the writer could improve in this piece?

    _____

7. Is there anything you wish the writer would include—an idea, an example, a specific detail?

    _____

8. Any additional comments about the writing:_____

    _____

    _____

    _____

    _____

Choosing Your Words

You've been learning how to choose words correctly: the correct pronoun to match a noun, the correct verb to agree with a subject. However, good writing is more than choosing the *correct* word. It also means choosing the *best* word.

The best word—

- expresses exactly what you mean
- helps your reader picture your ideas
- is appropriate for your reader
- adds to the rhythm of the writing

Your choice of words counts on the GED Writing Test. Just look at the scoring guide on page 192. You'll see that a high-scoring essay shows "varied and precise word choice."

Varied means "different." You don't use the same word over and over again. *Precise* means "exact, specific." You use a word that pinpoints your meaning. Your reader can understand exactly what you mean.

Here is an example of an essay topic you might find on the GED Writing Test:

TOPIC

Good leaders must have certain qualities.

In an essay, identify the qualities that good leaders have. Use your personal observations, knowledge, and experiences to support your ideas.

Here are two sample paragraphs on that topic. The second paragraph uses more varied and precise word choice. Which paragraph do you "get more out of" as a reader? That is, which paragraph makes a greater impact on you?

Weak word choice:

    A good leader gives confidence. People know that jobs will get done. They know that problems will get solved. They also know that goals will get done. Our mayor, for example, gives this kind of confidence.

Varied, precise word choice:

    A good leader inspires confidence. People know that work will be accomplished. They feel certain that problems will be solved. They are sure that goals will be reached. Our mayor, for example, creates such confidence wherever he goes.

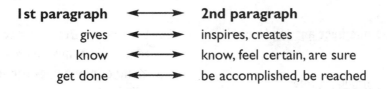

Compare some of the words used in those paragraphs:

1st paragraph	⟷	2nd paragraph
gives	⟷	inspires, creates
know	⟷	know, feel certain, are sure
get done	⟷	be accomplished, be reached

The words in the first paragraph are simple and rather vague. The words in the second paragraph are specific and sound more mature. These words—

- express exactly what the writer means
- help you picture the confidence of the people
- are appropriate for a GED essay reader
- add to the rhythm of the writing

To choose the best word, you need many different words at your fingertips. That can mean in your head. "At your fingertips" can also mean in a handy reference book, such as a dictionary or thesaurus. Of course, you cannot have such a book when you write your GED essay. However, you can and should use such books as you prepare for it! You can also learn and know more words just by reading and listening.

GED ESSAY PRACTICE

CHOOSE YOUR WORDS

1. **Read the paragraph below. Pay attention to the writer's choice of words. Rewrite the paragraph to improve them.**

    Another thing good leaders have is courage. Good leaders have the courage to say what they believe. Then they have to have the courage to stand behind what they believe. They can't go back and forth and always be changing their minds.

    _____

    _____

    _____

2. **Write a paragraph of your own on the topic about good leaders, given on page 116. Use varied and precise word choice.**

3. **Take a piece of writing from your portfolio. Revise it to improve your word choice.**

Writing models start on page 184.
For more practice with word choice, see page 159.

Choose the <u>one best answer</u> to each question.

<u>Questions 1 through 4</u> refer to the following business letter.

To Our Valued Customers:

(A)

(1) This is to inform you that WeePort Transport Company will make some changes in operations beginning immediately. (2) Due to rising costs, the fees for all transportation is being increased 10 percent. (3) Please understand that this increase is unavoidable.

(B)

(4) Because new safety regulations have been set, another change in our operations took place within the month. (5) As of October 1, we cannot allow a child to board the van unless him or her is accompanied by a parent. (6) Also, only riders with valid contracts will be allowed to board.

(C)

(7) We at WeePort plan to continue the excellent service you and your family expects. (8) Thank you for your understanding.

Sincerely,
Jerome Woods, Director

I. Sentence 2: **Due to rising costs, the fees for all transportation is being increased 10 percent.**

Which correction should be made to sentence 2?
(1) change <u>is</u> to <u>was</u>
(2) change <u>is</u> to <u>are</u>
(3) change <u>is</u> to <u>were</u>
(4) remove <u>being</u>
(5) no correction is necessary

2. Sentence 4: **Because new safety regulations have been set, another change in our operations took place within the month.**

Which correction should be made to sentence 2?
(1) change <u>have</u> to <u>has</u>
(2) remove <u>have</u>
(3) change <u>took</u> to <u>taking</u>
(4) change <u>took</u> to <u>will take</u>
(5) no correction is necessary

3. Sentence 5: **As of October 1, we cannot allow a child to board the van unless <u>him or her</u> is accompanied by a parent.**

Which is the best way to write the underlined portion of this sentence? If the original is the best way, choose option (1).
(1) him or her
(2) he or her
(3) he or she
(4) they
(5) them

4. Sentence 7: **We at WeePort plan to continue the excellent service you and your family <u>expects.</u>**

Which is the best way to write the underlined portion of this sentence? If the original is the best way, choose option (1).
(1) expects
(2) expected
(3) will expect
(4) have expected
(5) expect

Questions 5 through 8 refer to the following informative writing.

(A)

(1) According to the latest issue of *Consumer Computer Report*, there is some new ways to save time and money. (2) In addition, computer owners can cut down on your paper usage and help the environment as well. (3) If you're tired of spending money on reams and reams of paper and then spending too much time waiting for documents to print, read on.

(B)

(4) New Tech Company have introduced an inexpensive printing accessory that works with most desktop publishing software. (5) This accessory allows for printing top-quality two-sided documents automatically from a personal computer. (6) Neither the installation instructions nor the program are difficult to follow.

(C)

(7) Also, a new program that will help clean up hard drives is being planned for release next month. (8) It promises to save time on computer maintenance.

5. Sentence 1: **According to the latest issue of *Consumer Computer Report*, there is some new ways to save time and money.**

   Which correction should be made to sentence 1?
   (1) replace <u>there</u> with <u>here</u>
   (2) change <u>is</u> to <u>was</u>
   (3) change <u>is</u> to <u>are</u>
   (4) change <u>save</u> to <u>saving</u>
   (5) no correction is necessary

6. Sentence 2: **In addition, computer owners can cut down on your paper usage and help the environment as well.**

   Which correction should be made to sentence 2?
   (1) insert <u>they</u> after <u>owners</u>
   (2) change <u>can</u> to <u>could</u>
   (3) replace <u>your</u> with <u>their</u>
   (4) change <u>help</u> to <u>helps</u>
   (5) no correction is necessary

7. Sentence 4: **New Tech Company <u>have introduced</u> an inexpensive printing accessory that works with most desktop publishing software.**

   Which is the best way to write the underlined portion of this sentence? If the original is the best way, choose option (1).
   (1) have introduced
   (2) has introduced
   (3) introducing
   (4) introduce
   (5) being introduced

8. Sentence 6: **Neither the installation instructions nor the program <u>are</u> difficult to follow.**

   Which is the best way to write the underlined portion of this sentence? If the original is the best way, choose option (1).
   (1) are
   (2) were
   (3) be
   (4) being
   (5) is

Answers and explanations start on page 184.

Spelling, Punctuation, and Capitalization

LESSON GOALS

WRITING SKILLS

- Spell homonyms, possessives, and contractions correctly
- Correctly use end punctuation and commas to strengthen your writing
- Learn the rules of capitalization

WRITER'S TOOL

- Finish your portfolio

GED ESSAY CONNECTION

- Edit your essay

GED REVIEW

EXTRA PRACTICE, pp. 160–163

- Spell Well
- Punctuation
- Capitalization
- GED Essay

1. Think About the Topic

You are about to watch the program on *Spelling, Punctuation, and Capitalization*. This video will give you tips for learning spelling as well as some basic rules of punctuation and capitalization.

Throughout this video, writing teachers and professional writers discuss the importance of these "mechanics" of English. They explain how these areas reflect on the writer. They also explain how punctuation in particular can be used to make your writing clearer. One writer in the video refers to punctuation as "the spice of writing." What do you think she means by this?

2. Prepare to Watch the Video

A teacher in this program talks about homonyms. These are words that sound the same but are spelled differently. Homonyms cause spelling problems for many people. Write a sentence or two using this pair of homonyms: *no* and *know*. Make sure you use and spell each one correctly. Have someone else check your work.

_____

_____

You may have written something similar to this: *There was <u>no</u> way for me to <u>know</u> that you were there.*

3. Preview the Questions

Read the questions under *Think About the Program* on the next page and keep them in mind as you watch the program. After you watch, use the questions to review the main ideas in the program.

4. Study the Vocabulary

Review the terms to the right. Understanding the meaning of writing vocabulary will help you understand the video and the rest of the lesson.

WATCH THE PROGRAM

As you watch the program, pay special attention to the host who introduces or summarizes major ideas that you need to learn about. The host will also tell you important information about the GED Writing Test.

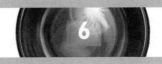

AFTER YOU WATCH

1. Think About the Program

How can you use punctuation to change the tone or meaning of a sentence?

What are some common forms of punctuation and their uses?

Why does a piece of writing with a lot of spelling mistakes reflect poorly on the writer?

Why is it important to be careful when using spell-check on a computer?

2. Make the Connection

In this program, you heard people discuss mnemonics. These are tricks people use to help them remember how to spell words. One such mnemonic is "*i* before *e* except after *c*." Write one word that you have difficulty spelling. Then see if you can develop a mnemonic to help you spell it correctly.

TERMS

apostrophe—a punctuation mark used in a possessive or a contraction

comma—a punctuation mark used to separate ideas and signal pauses in sentences

common noun—a noun that is the general name of a person, place, thing, or idea

contraction—a word made by combining two words and using an apostrophe to show where letters have been omitted

end punctuation—the mark put at the end of a sentence: period, exclamation point, or question mark

homonym—a word that sounds the same as another but is spelled differently

possessive—a word that shows ownership

proper noun—a noun that names a specific person, place, or thing and is always capitalized

"Spelling errors are like going out with stains on your shirt. . . . If a person looks at your letter and sees a misspelling, they're going to think you're sloppy."

Spelling

Homonyms

A **homonym** is a word that sounds the same as another word but is spelled differently. Using the wrong homonym is one of the most common spelling errors. That's why homonyms are tested on the GED Writing Test.

As you may remember from the video, even the spell-check tool on a computer cannot prevent a writer from using the wrong homonym. The only way to avoid homonym errors is to—

- learn the differences between homonyms, and
- edit your writing carefully

For example, suppose you know that *hear* means "to listen" and *here* means "in this place." Then you can catch the error in the sentence below:

When the new employees are hear, we'll start the training.

The writer should have used the homonym *here*, rather than *hear*.

The following chart lists some common homonyms.

Homonyms	Word Meanings	Example Uses
brake break	to stop; a device that stops to split apart; rest time	Put your foot on the brake. Please don't break any plates.
for four	meant to belong to the number 4	I made breakfast for you. The recipe requires four eggs.
knew new	past tense of *know* not old	I knew the secret yesterday. Troy bought a new motorcycle.
know no	to understand not any; opposite of *yes*	The repairmen know this system. They want no interference.
passed past	past tense of *pass* time before now; by and beyond	The van passed by hours ago. What do you know about the past?
right write	correct; opposite of *left* to put down words	This is the right way to handle it. You should write what you want.
through threw	into and out of; finished past tense of *throw*	We'll go through the rules once. She threw it away yesterday.
to two too	in the direction of the number 2 also; more than enough	Give it to me. You have two choices. The essay has too many errors.

The following words are not quite homonyms. However, they are often confused too.

Confusing Words	Word Meanings	Example Uses
accept except	to receive willingly excluding, but	We will accept your plan. Everyone except Mike likes the plan.
affect effect	to influence result	It did not affect me at all. What effect did the rain have?

SPELLING, PUNCTUATION & CAPITALIZATION ▪ PRACTICE 1

A. **Cross out each incorrect homonym below. Write the correct homonym above it.**

1. Your idea for speeding up work is knew, but it is two weeks too late.

2. When the shift is threw, we'll meet here in the break room.

3. There are for new workers on our shift.

4. Go through the two double doors, passed the office, and then turn right.

B. **Write a complete sentence using each word below.**

1. accept

   _____

2. except

   _____

3. affect

   _____

4. effect

   _____

C. **Read the sentence below and decide if all the words are spelled correctly. Then choose the <u>one best answer</u> to the question.**

   To demonstrate, the coach used two hands to toss the ball right threw the hoop.

   Which correction should be made to this sentence?
   (1) replace <u>two</u> with <u>to</u>
   (2) replace <u>two</u> with <u>too</u>
   (3) replace <u>right</u> with <u>write</u>
   (4) replace <u>threw</u> with <u>through</u>
   (5) no correction is necessary

Answers and explanations start on page 184.

Possessives

A **possessive** is a word that shows ownership. In a possessive noun, an **apostrophe** (')
shows the ownership. Follow these rules to write possessive nouns:

- To any singular noun or to a plural noun that does not end with -s, add 's:

  driver**'s** license   Barry**'s** home runs   boss**'s** temper   men**'s** clothing

- To a plural noun that ends with -s, add just the apostrophe: doctors' fees

Do you see how some possessive nouns and plurals sound alike?
For example:

> **Singular possessive:** That doctor's fees are high.
> **Plural possessive:** Those doctors' fees are high.
> **Plural:** Those doctors have high fees.

Pronouns can show possession too. A common spelling problem often shows up with
possessive pronouns. They are tricky because we sometimes think—incorrectly—that all
possessives need an apostrophe. Possessive pronouns *do not* need apostrophes:

> yours   his   hers   its   ours   theirs

To decide whether you need an apostrophe, ask yourself —
- Is this word a noun or a pronoun? If a pronoun—*no* apostrophe.
- Is this noun a possessive or just a plural? If just a plural—*no* apostrophe.
- Is this possessive noun singular or plural? If singular, add 's. If plural with -s,
  add '.

Contractions

A **contraction** is two words shortened into one. An apostrophe is used to show where
letters have been omitted:

> are not = aren't   I will = I'll

One spelling problem with contractions is putting the apostrophe in the wrong place. Be
sure you put it where the letters are missing, *not* where the two words were joined:

> did not = didn't   NOT   did'nt

Another spelling problem is one you've heard before—homonyms. Some contractions
and possessive pronouns are homonyms because they sound alike. For example:

Contraction	Possessive Pronoun
it's (it is *or* it has)	its (The dog gnaws its bone.)
you're (you are)	your (Give me your phone number.)
who's (who is *or* who has)	whose (Whose jacket is this?)

To decide whether to use the contraction or the possessive pronoun in a sentence, use this test:

- Substitute the words that make up the contraction.
- Ask yourself, *Does this sentence make sense?* If yes, use the contraction. If not, use the possessive pronoun.

For example, is it *Give it your best shot* or *Give it you're best shot? Give it you are best shot* makes no sense. Therefore, use the possessive pronoun *your*.

But that's not all. Here are *three* homonyms that can cause spelling fits:

Contraction	Possessive Pronoun	Adverb (Modifier)
they're (they are)	their (That is their home.)	there (Look over there!)

SPELLING, PUNCTUATION & CAPITALIZATION ■ PRACTICE 2

A. Cross out each misspelled possessive or contraction below. Write the correct spelling above it.

1. The decrepit old house was on it's last legs.

2. The owners put the house on the market because their moving south.

3. The neighbor's are wondering who's going to buy such a dismal home.

4. If your handy with a hammer and nail, this house is a buyer's bargain.

5. Its a shame the home's owners did not maintain it.

B. Write complete sentences using the following words.

1. they're _____

2. their _____

3. there _____

C. Read the sentence below and decide if all the words are spelled correctly. Then choose the one best answer to the question.

All past applicants were asked to send they're resumes and two letters of recommendation again.

Which correction should be made to this sentence?

(1) replace <u>past</u> with <u>passed</u>

(2) replace <u>they're</u> with <u>there</u>

(3) replace <u>they're</u> with <u>their</u>

(4) replace <u>two</u> with <u>too</u>

(5) no correction is necessary

Answers and explanations start on page 185.

For more practice with spelling, see page 160.

WRITING SKILLS

"Think of punctuation as a tool that you can use as a writer to make your writing more clear and to make it easier for the reader to follow what you have to say."

Punctuation

At the Ends of Sentences

You know how to write effective sentences. However, sentences can't be effective unless your reader knows where one ends and the next one begins. **End punctuation** is the mark you use to show that a sentence has ended.

- Use a period (.) at the end of a statement or an order:

  Our supervisor's vacation starts next week. Tell the rest of the staff that she'll be gone.

- Use a question mark (?) at the end of a question:

  When will she return?

- Use an exclamation point (!) to show strong emotion or force:

  She gets three whole weeks off! Wow!

Commas in a Series

The most common punctuation mark *within* a sentence is the **comma**. A comma separates ideas in a sentence. It also shows your reader where to pause.

For example, use commas in series in sentences. In a series, *more than two* items are listed, and the last item is connected with *and* or *or*. Place commas between the items:

These documents should not be <u>folded</u>, <u>stapled</u>, or <u>altered</u> in any way.

In that sentence, the three words in the series—*folded, stapled, altered*—are separated by commas. Read the sentence. You naturally pause after *folded* and *stapled*.

Be sure you are placing commas in a series of three or more. Don't use commas between just two items:

TVs and VCRs are in that department. We also sell phones and pagers.

Place commas correctly in the sentence below.

> The customer ordered coffee a bagel and cream cheese.

You should have put commas after *coffee* and *bagel*.

SPELLING, PUNCTUATION & CAPITALIZATION ■ PRACTICE 3

A. **Put a period, a question mark, an exclamation point, or a comma where one is needed in the sentences below.**

1. Yay Matt scored a perfect 300

2. A winning bowler needs good form a strong wrist and confidence

3. You also need to practice practice and practice some more

4. Matt Luis and Rey started bowling when they were teens

5. Where should we go to celebrate

B. **Write complete sentences that answer the questions below. Pay attention to correct punctuation.**

1. What are your three favorite foods?

   _____

2. What question would you like to ask the president?

   _____

3. Who are the four people you care most about in the world?

   _____

C. **Read the sentence below and decide if the punctuation is correct. Then choose the <u>one best answer</u> to the question.**

> The committee spent its time listening reading, and talking in order to fully understand the issue.

Which correction should be made to this sentence?

(1) insert a comma after <u>time</u>

(2) insert a comma after <u>listening</u>

(3) remove the comma after <u>reading</u>

(4) insert a comma after <u>understand</u>

(5) no correction is necessary

Answers and explanations start on page 185.

Commas in Compound and Complex Sentences

The teacher in the program explained two other uses of the comma. You might remember them from when you studied compound and complex sentences in Lesson 4.

■ Use a comma to separate the two complete thoughts in a compound sentence. The complete thoughts are called independent clauses. In the compound sentence below, a comma is used before the conjunction *but* to separate the independent clauses.

> I wanted to relax this weekend, but I had to help my brother move.

Remember that you need a conjunction along with the comma in a compound sentence. Otherwise, you create a comma splice—a mistake.

Overusing commas is a common error too. Can you tell why a comma is not needed in the sentence below? Look carefully at what comes before and after the conjunction *but*.

> I wanted to relax this weekend but had to help my brother move instead.

The conjunction *but* is not joining two independent clauses. Instead, *but* joins two verbs: *wanted* and *had*. If a writer placed a comma in that sentence, he or she would be overusing commas.

■ Use a comma to separate a dependent clause and an independent clause in a complex sentence when the dependent clause comes first. In the complex sentence below, a comma is used after the dependent clause beginning with the conjunction *Because*.

> Because my brother got a new job, he is moving to the other side of town.

Remember not to overuse commas! In general, a comma is *not* used when the dependent clause follows the independent clause:

> My brother is moving to the other side of town because he got a new job.

You can also use a comma after a long phrase at the beginning of a sentence. The comma tells your reader to pause. It helps show that the phrase is one piece of information in the sentence, separate from the main idea:

> Carrying furniture up two flights of stairs, I almost got a hernia!

Try this quick check on your comma know-how. Where would you put commas in these sentences?

> Even though employees are allowed sick days not everyone takes them.
> Our supervisor is very fair so most of us try to be here every day.

You should have placed a comma after *days* in the first sentence. That is the end of the dependent clause *Even though employee are allowed sick days*. You should have placed a comma after *fair* in the second sentence. The conjunction *so* joins two independent clauses in that compound sentence.

 SPELLING, PUNCTUATION & CAPITALIZATION ▪ PRACTICE 4

A. Put commas where they are needed in the sentences below. One sentence is correct as written.

1. Dealing with difficult customers is a skill and many people are not good at it.

2. Whenever a training session on this topic is held all employees must attend.

3. Patience is important if a customer starts to get angry or abusive.

4. Because our store values customer satisfaction employees should respond to all complaints quickly and respectfully.

5. By talking politely and calmly you can soothe most angry customers.

B. Write complete sentences using the conjunctions given. Use correct punctuation.

1. or _____

2. but _____

3. even though _____

4. while _____

C. Read the sentence below and decide if the punctuation is correct. Then choose the <u>one best answer</u> to the question.

You can always transfer a call to your manager, if you cannot satisfy a customer's complaint.

Which correction should be made to this sentence?

(1) insert a comma after <u>transfer</u>

(2) remove the comma after <u>manager</u>

(3) insert a comma after <u>if</u>

(4) insert a comma after <u>satisfy</u>

(5) no correction is necessary

Answers and explanations start on page 185.
For more practice with punctuation, see page 161.

"Proper nouns refer to specific people, places, and things, and that tends to be where the capital letters come in."

Capitalization

Basic Capitalization Rules

In the video, you learned three basic rules for capitalizing. Here's a quick review:

- Always capitalize the first word in a sentence.

  Saving money can be challenging, but it is important to do.

- Capitalize the pronoun *I* no matter where it is in a sentence.

  My plan is to put part of every dollar I earn into a savings account.

- Capitalize a noun that names a specific person, place, or thing.

  The best interest rate right now is at Downtown Federal Savings.

The first two rules above are easy to follow. The third rule can sometimes be tricky. The name *Downtown Federal Savings* needs to be capitalized because it is not naming just any bank—it names a specific bank. In other words, it is a proper noun.

Common and Proper Nouns

A **common noun** is one that names a *general* person, place, or thing. For example:

woman   man   street   city   organization   corporation   day   month   war

Common nouns are not capitalized unless they begin a sentence.

A **proper noun** is one that names a *specific* person, place, or thing. Proper nouns are capitalized. Compare the common nouns and the proper nouns in the chart below:

Common Noun	Proper Noun
woman, man	Mrs. Rose Ortega, Dr. Martin Luther King, Jr.
street	First Street
city	Atlantic City
organization	National Organization for Women
corporation	Sony Corporation
day, month	Tuesday, September
house	the White House
war	Persian Gulf War

A. **Correct the errors in capitalization below. Draw three lines under each lowercase letter that should be a capital letter, like this: i.**

1. asking your employer for direct deposit of your paycheck is a great idea.

2. My employer, the healthy pet food company, deposits my check into my checking account.

3. On friday i record the deposit in my checkbook.

4. I live in boston, massachusetts, and the taxes alone here require me to be as careful as possible with my money.

5. Remember that the boston tea party was all about taxes too!

B. **Write complete sentences to answer the following questions. Capitalize correctly.**

1. Where and when were you born?

   _____

2. What is the name of your school or place of employment?

   _____

3. What is your favorite brand of toothpaste?

   _____

4. What is the name of a local sports team?

   _____

5. At which stores do you shop?

   _____

C. **Read the sentence below and decide if capital letters are used correctly. Then choose the <u>one best answer</u> to the question.**

The manager at Allstate Construction Supplies oversees the delivery of lumber the third Monday of every month.

Which correction should be made to this sentence?

(1) change <u>manager</u> to <u>Manager</u>

(2) change <u>Allstate Construction Supplies</u> to <u>allstate construction supplies</u>

(3) change <u>Monday</u> to <u>monday</u>

(4) change <u>month</u> to <u>Month</u>

(5) no correction is necessary

Answers and explanations start on page 185.

WRITING SKILLS

To Capitalize or Not to Capitalize?

Remember the narrator in the program? He said that keeping straight which nouns are proper can be confusing. That's why most of us tend to overcapitalize. We use capital letters when they are not really needed.

Here are some rules for when *not* to capitalize:

- Do not capitalize the seasons of the year:

  summer   fall   autumn   winter   spring

- Do not capitalize a term of family relationship—*mother, grandpa, uncle*—when it is used only with a possessive pronoun:

  My uncle is visiting from Canada.

However, do capitalize it when it is used right before the person's name or when you are addressing that person directly:

  My Uncle Chuck is visiting from Canada.
  How do you like the United States, Uncle?

- People's titles often give people trouble. Do not capitalize a title—*president, senator, coach, doctor, captain*—when it is used alone:

  The captain of the ship spoke to the crew and passengers.

However, do capitalize a title when it is used right before the person's name or when you are addressing that person directly:

  His name was Captain Andrews.
  Aye, aye, Captain!

- Do not capitalize a geographic feature—*lake, river, mountain*—or a structure—*street, building, monument*—when it is used alone.

  The highway runs along the river in the city.

However, do capitalize it when it is part of a name that you could find on a map.

  The West Side Highway runs along the Hudson River in New York City.

Remember: You must have a specific reason to capitalize a word in a sentence. Otherwise, don't capitalize it.

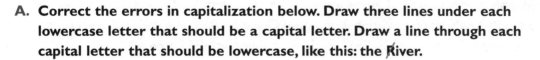
A. Correct the errors in capitalization below. Draw three lines under each lowercase letter that should be a capital letter. Draw a line through each capital letter that should be lowercase, like this: the ~~R~~iver.

1. Believe it or not, going to an Art Gallery can be stress-relieving and relaxing.

2. Many museums in Cities are open late on thursdays for people who work weekdays.

3. In fact, there is often no Entry Fee if you arrive after six o'clock in the Evening.

4. For a relaxing visit, don't try to see every single painting by a master Artist like picasso.

5. The museum I enjoy most in the World is in washington, d.c., and is called the national museum of african art.

B. Write complete sentences to answer the following questions. Capitalize correctly.

1. What is your favorite museum, park, or movie theater?

   _____

2. What are three activities you enjoy in your free time?

   _____

3. Who is one of your favorite family members, and what relation is he or she to you?

   _____

4. Which day of the week do you like the least, and which season is your favorite?

   _____

C. Read the sentence below and decide if capital letters are used correctly. Then choose the <u>one best answer</u> to the question.

   When Coach Liccardi is on the field, every member of the Team pays attention.

Which correction should be made to this sentence?
   (1) change <u>Coach</u> to <u>coach</u>
   (2) change <u>Liccardi</u> to <u>liccardi</u>
   (3) change <u>member</u> to <u>Member</u>
   (4) change <u>Team</u> to <u>team</u>
   (5) no correction is necessary

Answers and explanations start on page 185.
For more practice with capitalization, see page 162.

Finishing Your Portfolio—A Writer's Reflection

By now, you have several pieces of writing in your portfolio. Congratulations! As you certainly know by now, writing is not always easy. It takes time, thought, and effort. However, it is always rewarding. Just look at your portfolio for proof!

Now you are near the end of this workbook. Think about all the topics you have written. Here are some of them:

- Journal writing
- Writing your own personal story
- Stress
- Honesty
- Television

- A Sunday afternoon
- A time you learned something
- Heroes
- Work
- Leadership

Think also about the many skills you have worked on. Here are a few of them:

- Getting ideas
- Organizing ideas
- Writing a first draft
- Revising
- Editing
- Writing a topic sentence
- Supporting a topic sentence

- Writing a compare/contrast piece
- Writing a pro/con piece
- Introducing and concluding
- Combining sentences
- Choosing words carefully
- Using correct grammar
- Using the mechanics of English

As you worked on each skill, you added to your writing portfolio. Whether you were aware of it or not, your writing skills were improving along the way. Now is a good time to reflect on yourself as a writer.

To **reflect** means to read your work and think about what it means to you. Think how far you have come in your writing. Think also about where you want to go from here.

The form on the following page will help you reflect on your writing progress. To use the chart effectively, follow these steps:

1. Arrange your writing in the order in which the pieces were written. Feel free to include other writing you have done outside this workbook.

2. Take 10 to 20 minutes to read over your work. Pay attention to—

   - problems or errors that appear in earlier pieces but less so in later pieces
   - areas of strength or success, and where they occur in the range of your work

With your writing portfolio in front of you, complete the form on the next page.

A Writer's Reflection

by _____

What are one or two problems in your early writing that became less frequent in your later writing?

_____

_____

What is the biggest difference between the first piece you wrote and the last?

_____

_____

Which piece of writing did you enjoy working on the most? Why? Do you see any connection between writing you enjoyed doing and the quality of the writing?

_____

_____

_____

What are your goals for the future as a writer? Are there any specific skills you would like to develop?

_____

_____

How does writing make you feel? What kind of writer do you think you are?

_____

_____

Take out the chart you made on page 55 of this workbook. Would any of your answers be different now that you have spent more time working as a writer?

_____

_____

GED Essay Connection

Editing Your Essay

You know that the final step in the writing process is editing your work. When you edit, you find and correct errors in—

- sentence structure
- grammar and usage
- mechanics—spelling, punctuation, capitalization

Those are the skills you have practiced in the last three lessons.

Using Your Time Wisely

On the GED Writing Test, you will have 45 minutes to plan, write, revise, and edit your essay. That means you will have from 5 to 10 minutes to edit several paragraphs. Therefore, focus on editing the errors that most affect how easy it is to read your writing.

Also, you will not have time to copy your essay over. The essay scorers know that. They will not mind seeing editing marks like those shown on page 191 if the marks are neat. In fact, these marks will show the readers that you took the time to edit your work.

Here is an example of an essay topic you might find on the GED Writing Test. Read it carefully.

TOPIC

Is there such a thing as luck?

In an essay, explain whether you think some people have good luck or bad luck, or whether luck plays no role in people's lives. Use your personal observations, experience, and knowledge to support your essay.

The paragraph below is from an essay about that topic. Read the paragraph. See how the errors have been edited using the editing marks shown on page 191.

                          naturally

Some people do seem to be ~~natrally~~ lucky. I don't mean the kind of luck (they have) that's involved in winning the lottery. I mean they seem to land on their feet. Nothing too bad happens to them, ^At least not for long. My uncle Dave is like that. He lost his job in the factory, but he was selected for job retraining ~~and~~ now he has an even better, higher-paying job. *When* His girlfriend left him, ~~but then~~ her girlfriend Lupe ~~come~~ *came* to tell Dave how sorry she was, ~~and~~ now Dave and Lupe are happily married.

Start Practicing Now

In the program, a student writing tutor noted that editing errors is "something you get in time. . . . Eventually, it becomes second nature." Therefore, begin editing your writing as much as possible now. Use the following tools to help you so that they are second nature when you edit your GED essay:

- The Editing Checklist on page 191
- The editing marks shown on page 191
- Your Target Error List on page 53. Add new target errors if you need to. Cross out those that are no longer problems. Then copy your Target Error List onto a separate sheet of paper. When you edit, use it.

GED ESSAY PRACTICE

EDIT YOUR ESSAY

1. **Below is another paragraph from the essay based on the topic about luck. Edit the paragraph below using the Editing Checklist from page 191.**

   While people like my Uncle Dave seem to blessed with good luck other people seem to have nothing but bad luck. My sister, for example, has had a rough life. Last year is extremely tough on her. She was in a car accident. It was no fault of hers. Her teeth were knocked loose but even worse her eyes were damaged. Several months later she was eating at a fast-food restaurant, and got food poisoning. Ended up in the hospital for a weak. All this happened after she lost her job in that same factory that my Uncle had worked in.

2. Read the topic about luck on page 134 again. Write a paragraph on it below. Then edit your paragraph using the Editing Checklist and your Target Error List.

   _____

   _____

   _____

   _____

3. Take out a revised piece of writing from your portfolio. Edit the piece using the Editing Checklist and your Target Error List.

Answers start on page 186.
For more practice with editing an essay, see page 163.

GED Review: Spelling Punctuation & Capitalization

Choose the one best answer to each question.

Questions 1 through 4 refer to the following article.

(A)

(1) Is it true that an apple a day can keep the doctor away? (2) "Not always," says Dr. Harry Mintz, chief nutritionist at hillside medical center. (3) However, the doctor does say that apple's have extraordinary health and nutritional benefits that many people may be unaware of.

(B)

(4) For a relatively inexpensive and easy-to-eat food, an apple packs quite a wallop in terms of three crucial nutrients—fiber vitamins, and minerals. (5) For example, a medium-size apple contains just 70 calories, with virtually no fat or sodium. (6) Furthermore, the apple's antioxidants and fiber help to lower cholesterol levels, and protect against lung and colon cancer.

1. Sentence 2: **"Not always," says Dr. Harry Mintz, chief nutritionist at hillside medical center.**

   Which correction should be made to sentence 2?
   (1) change says to say's
   (2) insert a comma after says
   (3) change Dr. to dr.
   (4) change hillside medical center to Hillside Medical Center
   (5) no correction is necessary

2. Sentence 3: **However, the doctor does say that apple's have extraordinary health and nutritional benefits that many people may be unaware of.**

   Which correction should be made to sentence 3?
   (1) remove the comma after However
   (2) change doctor to Doctor
   (3) change does to do
   (4) insert a comma after say
   (5) change apple's to apples

3. Sentence 4: **For a relatively inexpensive and easy-to-eat food, an apple packs quite a wallop in terms of three crucial nutrients—fiber vitamins, and minerals.**

   Which is the best way to write the underlined portion of this sentence? If the original is the best way, choose option (1).
   (1) fiber vitamins, and minerals
   (2) fiber, vitamins, and minerals
   (3) fiber vitamins and minerals
   (4) fiber, vitamins and, minerals
   (5) fiber, vitamins, and, minerals

4. Sentence 6: **Furthermore, the apple's antioxidants and fiber help to lower cholesterol levels, and protect against lung and colon cancer.**

   Which correction should be made to sentence 6?
   (1) change apple's to apples
   (2) change help to helps
   (3) replace to with two
   (4) remove the comma after levels
   (5) insert a comma after lung

Questions 5 through 8 refer to the following letter.

Dear Mrs. Anderson:

(A)

(1) We at South Cove Child Learning Center would like to report on the progress of your daughter, Felicia, here at school. (2) She is a happy and bright child, and the staff just adores her. (3) When we excepted her eight months ago, we knew she would become an important part of our community.

(B)

(4) Felicia has many friends here at South Cove—especially Devon and Makayla. (5) Even though Felicia is almost a year younger than these two children she can keep up with them with no trouble. (6) However, they're is always room for improvement, and we are trying to get Felicia to share more often and keep her voice down during circle time.

(C)

(7) When she is engaged in the Classroom activities, Felicia and her friends do well. (8) Her fine motor skills are excellent, and she is one of our top singers and dancers! (9) Please feel free to call us with any questions.

5. Sentence 3: **When we excepted her eight months ago, we knew she would become an important part of our community.**

Which correction should be made to sentence 3?
(1) replace excepted with accepted
(2) replace eight with ate
(3) remove the comma after ago
(4) replace knew with new
(5) insert a comma after knew

6. Sentence 5: **Even though Felicia is almost a year younger than these two children she can keep up with them with no trouble.**

Which correction should be made to sentence 5?
(1) replace two with to
(2) replace two with too
(3) insert a comma after children
(4) insert a comma after them
(5) no correction is necessary

7. Sentence 6: **However, they're is always room for improvement, and we are trying to get Felicia to share more often and keep her voice down during circle time.**

Which correction should be made to sentence 6?
(1) replace they're with there
(2) replace they're with their
(3) remove the comma after improvement
(4) insert a comma after often
(5) insert a comma after down

8. Sentence 7: **When she is engaged in the Classroom activities, Felicia and her friends do well.**

Which correction should be made to sentence 7?
(1) insert a comma after engaged
(2) change Classroom to classroom
(3) remove the comma after activities
(4) replace friends with friend's
(5) no correction is necessary

Answers and explanations start on page 186.

WRITING PRACTICE

Free Writing, pages 22–23

Remember these things when you free write:

- Don't worry about spelling, punctuation, or grammar.
- You don't have to correct anything you have written.
- Time yourself, and keep writing until the time is up.

A. **Look at the picture. What do you see? How do you feel? Where does your mind go when you look at this scene? Spend five minutes free writing about your thoughts.**

_____

_____

_____

_____

_____

_____

_____

_____

_____

_____

_____

_____

_____

_____

_____

_____

_____

B. **On another sheet of paper, spend five minutes free writing about whatever comes into your head when you think about the topic below.**

Having Lots of Money

To check your answers, see page 186.

Letters and E-Mail, pages 26–29

A. **Write a short personal letter to a friend or relative. You can write about something you have done recently, something that happened to you, or anything else you choose.**

Write your address on the first two lines and the date on the last line.

_____
_____
_____

Dear _____,

_____
_____
_____
_____
_____
_____
_____
_____
_____
_____
_____
_____
_____

B. **Write an e-mail message to a different friend or relative. If you do not know a real e-mail address, make up one using the person's first initial and last name.**

To: _____@mindlink.com

Subject: _____

To check your answers, see page 186.

Personal Stories, pages 30–33

A. Think about the time line below as your life so far. Choose three different ages on the line and put an X at each spot.

BIRTH   2   4   6   8   10   12   14   16   18   ...   PRESENT

Now in each box below, record one age you chose. In that box, jot down one or two significant events that happened to you at that age.

Age _____

_____
_____
_____
_____

Age _____

_____
_____
_____
_____

Age _____

_____
_____
_____
_____

B. Choose one event you recorded above. Jot down more details about the event. On another sheet of paper, write a personal story about it. Remember to do the following:

■ Set the stage (beginning).
■ Describe the action (middle).
■ Look back (end).

To check your answers, see page 186.

GED Essay: Development and Details, pages 36–37

> ### TOPIC
>
> How important are cooperation and teamwork in life?
>
> In an essay, explain your point of view on cooperation and teamwork. Use your personal observations, knowledge, and experiences to support your essay.

A. **Below are general statements about the topic. Add these kinds of details for each statement:**

- **examples that show teamwork in the situation**
- **reasons that support or explain why it is important in the situation**
- **specific information that helps a reader picture teamwork in the situation**

   1. **Teamwork is important among family members.**

_____

_____

_____

   2. **Teamwork is important on the job.**

_____

_____

_____

   3. **Teamwork is important in a good marriage.**

_____

_____

_____

B. **Write a piece about the topic of teamwork. Use the ideas and details you wrote in Part A above. Add new ones if you can.**

_____

_____

_____

_____

_____

To check your answers, see page 186.

Brainstorm and Cluster, pages 42–45

A. In each box below, write down the first five thoughts that come to mind when you read the topic inside. Remember: There are no "wrong" or "silly" ideas when you brainstorm!

Renting an apartment or house

1. _____
2. _____
3. _____
4. _____
5. _____

World peace

1. _____
2. _____
3. _____
4. _____
5. _____

B. Use the cluster below to think about growing old. Start by writing ideas in the circles and connecting them to the topic or to each other. Then add circles and ideas, and connect them in any way that makes sense.

GROWING OLD

To check your answers, see page 186.

Outline, pages 48–49

A. **Organize the ideas below into an outline. Some information has already been filled in. Write your own thesis statement and second supporting idea.**

Credit Cards

good because safer than carrying cash

too easy to make impulse purchases

finance charges can be ridiculously high

helpful when ordering over the phone

can use easily to order online

my brother is over $10,000 in debt on his card

can help you keep track of purchases

many people misuse them, get into financial trouble

some credit card companies take advantage

Thesis: _____

Supporting Idea 1: Some positive things about credit cards

   a.   good because safer than carrying cash _____

   _____

   _____

   _____

Supporting Idea 2: _____

   a.   too easy to make impulse purchases _____

   _____

   _____

   _____

B. **On a separate sheet of paper, write an outline using the ideas written below. Remember to write a thesis statement and clear supporting ideas. Add other details to your outline if you like.**

dogs are affectionate and loyal

dogs love to lie at your feet or in your lap

cats are more independent—great for people not home a lot

cats don't require as much attention or time

snakes easy to care for, stay in confined area

dogs require training, walking outside

snakes are fascinating

To check your answers, see page 186.

Revise and Edit, pages 50–53

A. Choose a piece of writing that has not been revised or edited yet. It could be the piece about cooperation and teamwork that you wrote on page 143. Revise your writing using the questions below and the marks on page 191 in the Handbook.

1. What is the thesis or main idea of your writing?

   _____

   _____

2. Is it stated clearly? If not, rewrite the thesis or main idea statement here.

   _____

   _____

3. Add one sentence that gives your writing more support or detail. Write the sentence here. Then indicate with an insert mark, or caret, where it should go in the piece of writing. (See page 191 for an example of inserting with a caret.)

   _____

   _____

4. Does the order of ideas make sense, or should an idea be moved? If you need to move an idea, use an arrow to show where.

5. Can you make new paragraphs by dividing one long paragraph? If so, use a paragraph mark to show where. (See page 191 for an example of using a paragraph mark.)

6. Cross out any sentence that does not belong.

B. Use the same piece of writing to practice your editing skills. Follow the steps below.

7. Read each sentence separately and aloud. Circle errors you hear. Are all sentences complete, or do you hear any fragments? Are there any run-on sentences? Correct the errors you circled.

8. Now pay attention to the verbs. Circle errors you hear. Do the verbs agree with the subjects? Are they the correct form and tense? Correct the errors you circled.

9. Finally, find and correct any errors in—

   - spelling
   - capitalization
   - punctuation

To check your answers, see page 187.

GED Essay: Respond to the Topic, pages 56–57

TOPIC

What personal quality is most important to being successful at work?

In an essay, tell what the quality is and why you think it is important. Use your personal observations, knowledge, and experience to support your essay.

A. **Read each thesis statement below. Decide if it answers the topic question above. Write *yes* or *no* in the blank.**

_____ 1. "It is necessary to work in order to get by in today's society."

_____ 2. "People must have problem-solving skills in order to be successful at work."

_____ 3. "The ability to work with all kinds of people is most important for success on the job."

_____ 4. "Working successfully is challenging to most people."

B. **Now work on responding to the topic in your own way by following these steps.**

5. Write down a quality that you think answers the topic question.

_____

6. Brainstorm for three minutes to get some ideas about the quality and why you think it answers the topic question.

_____

_____

_____

_____

_____

_____

_____

7. Study the ideas you noted above. Write a thesis statement here.

_____

_____

8. Read the question in the topic assignment. Then read your thesis statement. Does it answer the topic question?

To check your answers, see page 187.

Topic Sentences, pages 62–65

Remember these things about good topic sentences:

- A topic sentence tells what the main idea of a paragraph is.
- A topic sentence clues the reader about what will follow.
- A topic sentence is not too general and not too specific.

A. All the sentences below are related to the topic of honesty. Match the topic sentence on the left with the paragraph it belongs with on the right. Write the letter of the paragraph before the number of its topic sentence.

_____ 1. I have never been honest with my father.

a. For example, if a friend asks you what you think about something important, you may feel like lying to avoid hurting him or her. However, being honest with people is a sign of respect. Being dishonest might seem kind at first, but in the end the truth is most valuable in a relationship.

_____ 2. Honesty is a quality that many people do not exhibit.

b. When I was a boy, I would lie about things I did. When he asked me what I thought about something, I would say what I thought he wanted to hear instead of the truth. Even now I tell "white lies" in order not to hurt him.

_____ 3. Honesty can sometimes be difficult, but it is usually the best course of action.

c. For some reason, many people find it difficult to face up to the facts and represent them clearly. Instead, they'd rather beat around the bush and avoid real, honest dialogue. The last three men I dated all lied to me at crucial times in our relationship.

B. Read the paragraph below, and write a topic sentence for it. Be sure to keep in mind the guidelines above.

_____

_____

I tell my friends the truth because I know that is what they expect of me. I do not lie to my husband and my children because they want to know the "real me"—not some phony. I am honest with my coworkers and my boss because we respect each other and need the truth in order to work effectively.

To check your answers, see page 187.

Organized Paragraphs, pages 66–69

Remember these ways to organize a paragraph:

Sequence	Pros and Cons	Compare and Contrast
events in time order; what happened first, second, and so on	the good side of something, the bad side, or both	what is the same and what is different about two people, things, or ideas
Transition words: *first, when, next, finally, once, then, before, after, in the beginning, in the end*	Transition words: *however, on the other hand, but, moreover, in addition, furthermore*	Transition words: Compare—*likewise, similarly, also, too* Contrast—*on the other hand, in contrast, nevertheless, however, but*

A. Choose one of the following topics and ways of organizing ideas to write a paragraph. Generate ideas on another sheet of paper. Then write an organized paragraph below. Use transition words to show your organization.

- What is the funniest thing that ever happened to you? (sequence)
- What are the advantages and disadvantages of having a telephone? (pros and cons)
- How are you the same as when you were a child, and how have you changed? (compare and contrast)

_____

_____

_____

_____

_____

_____

_____

_____

_____

_____

_____

B. Choose a second topic to write about and a method of organization. Write a paragraph on another sheet of paper.

To check your answers, see page 187.

Divide and Combine Paragraphs, pages 70–73

A. **Revise the writing below by dividing it into four paragraphs. Use the paragraph mark to show where each new paragraph should begin.**

There are two ways to get a job done well. One way is to do it yourself so that you have control over every aspect of the work. Another way is to find people to help so that you take advantage of other people's skills, energy, and talent. Both methods have advantages and disadvantages. If you decide to get the job done by yourself, you do not have to depend on other people. Therefore, other people's mistakes, laziness, lateness, or incompetence will never be a problem for you. However, you need to have lots of time and energy to get the job done on your own. In addition, you will not get another person's opinions, which can be valuable in doing a job well. If you decide to get people to help you with the job, there are entirely different advantages and disadvantages. First of all, you give up control of the work. Different people have different ideas about how to get a job done, and you'll have to give your helpers some input. A clear advantage to getting help, of course, is that the work is spread out among more people, thus saving you time and energy. These two methods for getting a job done well can both work. Deciding which method to use—working alone or with others—depends on which pros and cons you want to deal with!

B. **This set of directions should have only four paragraphs. Draw a line from the end of one paragraph to the beginning of the next if the two paragraphs should be combined into one.**

The procedures for opening the coffee shop are outlined below. Please be sure you understand them and are able to complete all the tasks. If you have any questions or concerns, please contact the day supervisor.

Your first priority is store entrance. Use your key and the coded keypad to enter the shop. Be sure to lock the doors once you are inside; the shop is not open for customers until 8:00.

Your next focus should be on set-up. Be sure the floor has been swept by the night crew. If it has not, a dust mop can be found in the cleaning supply locker.

Remove chairs from tabletops and set them up at tables. Set napkin holders, salt and pepper shakers, and sugars out on each table.

Next, start the food preparation. Six coffee pots should be started, including two decaffeinated.

Heat the grills to 350 degrees. Stock the shelves with bread and rolls from the delivery bin. Remove eggs, butter, and milk from the walk-in refrigerator, and arrange mixing bowls so that the cook can get right to work when she arrives.

To check your answers, see page 187.

GED Essay: Write an Introduction and Conclusion, pages 76–77

Use this topic and your work from page 147 to answer the questions that follow.

> ### TOPIC
>
> What personal quality is most important to being successful at work?
>
> In an essay, tell what the quality is and why you think it is important. Use your personal observations, knowledge, and experience to support your essay.

A. **Write an introduction for an essay on the topic above. Use the ideas you came up with on page 147. You may also want to add some new ones.**

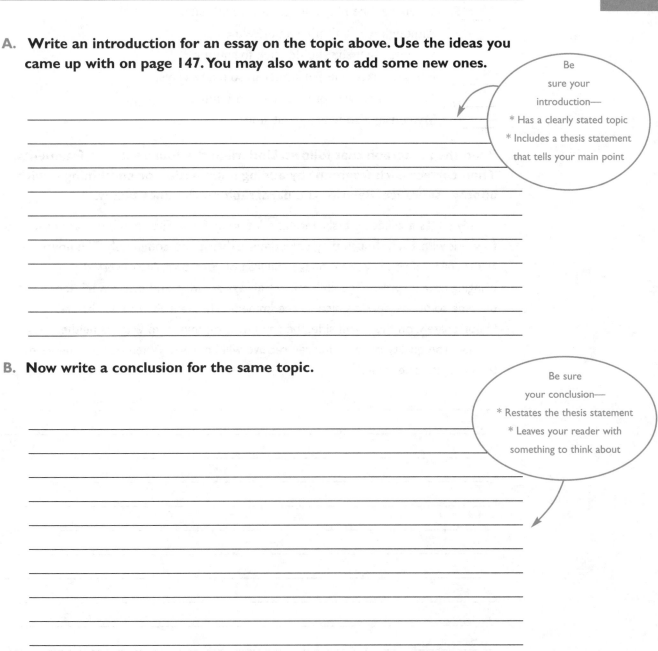

Be sure your introduction—
* Has a clearly stated topic
* Includes a thesis statement that tells your main point

B. **Now write a conclusion for the same topic.**

Be sure your conclusion—
* Restates the thesis statement
* Leaves your reader with something to think about

To check your answers, see page 187.

Complete Sentences, pages 82–85

Remember these facts about complete sentences:

- A complete sentence has a subject.
- A complete sentence has a predicate.
- A complete sentence tells a complete thought.

A. Write *C* in the blank if the group of words is a complete sentence. Write *F* if it is a fragment.

_____ 1. Whenever she plays the guitar, we all laugh.

_____ 2. Although we can't play a note either.

_____ 3. We agree that she should stick to singing.

_____ 4. Being an excellent performer in so many ways.

_____ 5. The last time we got together as a family.

_____ 6. My cousin also tells a great story.

B. Read the paragraph that follows. Underline the four sentence fragments. Then correct each fragment by adding information or combining it with another sentence. Rewrite the paragraph on the lines below.

My job as a childcare assistant has a lot going for it. First of all, kids are neat to work with. Even though they sometimes exhaust you completely. The hours are excellent if you have school-age children of your own. Also, every day bringing new surprises. The children are always growing, and every week they become someone new. It's nice to see immediately the fruits of your labors. Unfortunately, on the down side, the pay. Living on minimum wage is neither easy nor fair. The quality of care children receive will improve. When our pay increases to reflect its true value.

_____

_____

_____

_____

_____

_____

_____

_____

_____

_____

_____

To check your answers, see page 187.

Compound Sentences, pages 86–87

Remember how to write a compound sentence:
- Write a simple sentence.
- Add a comma and a FANBOYS conjunction—*for, and, nor, but, or, yet,* or *so.*
- Add another simple, related sentence.

A. **Create compound sentences by combining each pair of simple sentences. Use commas and FANBOYS conjunctions.**

1. Time is running short. Live life to the fullest.

   _____

2. We wanted to buy a house. We can afford only to rent right now.

   _____

3. Sam will have a cheeseburger. Natalie wants a chicken sandwich.

   _____

4. Eat, drink, and be merry. Tomorrow we may die.

   _____

5. You can finish the dishes tonight. You can leave them until the morning.

   _____

B. **Create compound sentences by adding another simple sentence to each simple sentence below. Use commas and FANBOYS conjunctions.**

6. It's going to rain tonight _____

   _____

7. My brother and his wife want tickets to that concert _____

   _____

8. You did an excellent job _____

9. Ms. Zerfas is the new supervisor on the night shift _____

   _____

10. You can use the computer at the library to send and receive e-mail

    _____

To check your answers, see page 187.

Complex Sentences, pages 90–91

A. Create complex sentences by combining each pair of independent and dependent clauses. If you put the dependent clause at the beginning of the sentence, remember to put a comma after it. (There is more than one correct way to write the complex sentences.)

1. he will not receive a raise this year
   if his work does not improve

   _____

2. because my son is quite tall for his age
   the basketball coach wants him to try out

   _____

3. I almost always eat dessert
   after I finish my dinner

   _____

4. unless you have a better idea
   we'll go to the movies tonight

   _____

5. the mice will play
   while the cat's away

   _____

B. Create complex sentences. If the clause is dependent, add a comma and an independent clause. If the clause is independent, add a dependent clause with an appropriate dependent conjunction.

6. Before you can take the GED Test _____

7. When I was young _____

8. I didn't like that movie at all _____

9. Wear appropriate clothes to a job interview _____

10. Although we've known each other for years _____

11. Heather got a tattoo on her shoulder _____

To check your answers, see page 188.

154

GED Essay: Vary Sentence Structure, pages 96–97

Remember these ways to improve the variety of your sentences:

- Combine ideas to make compound and complex sentences.
- Write long and short sentences.
- Ask a question.
- Add opening, closing, and renaming phrases.

A. Revise each group of sentences to add variety to the writing.

1. I like to eat out. My husband likes to eat at home. My kids like to eat at home. I'm the one who has to do all the cooking. This does not seem fair. No one is bothered except me. I'd like to think of a solution. My husband and children do not see the need for a solution. They do not see a problem.

   _____

   _____

   _____

   _____

2. Your report is excellent. It is complete. It has lots of interesting details. It raises some interesting points. The report was late. Two weeks is too long for the committee to wait for this kind of thing. We'd like to implement some of your suggestions. We are finding it difficult given the time constraints. It is too bad you did not deliver it on time. You will learn from this situation.

   _____

   _____

   _____

   _____

B. Look at the introduction and conclusion you wrote on page 151. On another sheet of paper, revise these paragraphs using the following guidelines.

3. See if you can combine sentences to make compound or complex sentences.

4. Write one short sentence in the introduction that adds emphasis to the paragraph.

5. Write a question in the conclusion that causes the reader to think.

To check your answers, see page 188.

Nouns and Pronouns, pages 102–105

A. **Underline the nouns in each sentence below. Circle each pronoun. Then draw an arrow from each pronoun to the noun it refers to (its antecedent).**

1. The weather forecaster predicted snow last night, and it appeared before midnight.

2. Mrs. Ortega, books are a wonderful gift for your granddaughter, so I suggest you order her a copy of *Pat the Bunny*.

3. Because the apples in the crate seem soft, please put them on the discount table.

4. My partner plans to take his vacation after mine this year.

5. The artist shows only his watercolors because he believes they are his only good work.

6. The teenager asked his parents for the car, but they said no to him.

B. **Choose the correct pronoun in parentheses, and write it in the blank.**

7. Our boss requires Lou Samels and (I, me) to arrive one-half hour before the other employees.

   _____

8. (He, Him) and I don't mind most of the time.

   _____

9. We need to do (we, us, our) share whenever we can.

   _____

10. The orders Mae processed had to be redone because (it, they, them) had lots of errors.

    _____

11. Time is money, our boss tells (we, us) employees.

    _____

12. He also promised a raise to Lou and (I, me) because of all the overtime we put in.

    _____

13. My boss and (I, me) get along pretty well.

    _____

To check your answers, see page 188.

Verb Tense, pages 106–107

A. Underline the correct verb in parentheses for each sentence below.

1. Last week the newspaper (will report, reported) the arrest of Bob Hollins.

2. Bob (was, will be) an employee at Riverside Health Center.

3. Before his arrest, most people (think, thought) that Bob was an honest worker.

4. It turns out that Bob (is, was) stealing money from residents and staff.

5. His theft (begins, began) over two years ago when he (worked, will work) on the geriatric floor.

6. He (is, was) stealing cash and jewelry while residents slept and the staff was busy elsewhere.

7. Currently, Bob (spent, spends) his days and nights at the county jail awaiting trial.

8. His sentencing (took, will take) place next June.

B. Write the correct form of the verb in parentheses in the blank.

9. We are glad that you (bring) your family with you tonight.

   _____

10. You (choose) to come to the restaurant on a quiet evening.

    _____

11. Last night there (be) many more diners here.

    _____

12. The staff and I have (think) of ways to make our customers feel welcome and comfortable.

    _____

13. I see that our host has seated you and has (give) you menus.

    _____

14. Has your waiter (take) your order yet?

    _____

To check your answers, see page 188.

Subject-Verb Agreement, pages 110–113

A. **Underline the subject in each sentence below. Then circle the correct verb in parentheses.**

1. My girlfriend and I usually (agree, agrees) to do something together every weekend.

2. Hiking, biking, and skating (is, are) some of the things we enjoy.

3. Occasionally, either she or I (decide, decides) to do something alone.

4. When this situation (arise, arises), the other one of us usually (stay, stays) home.

5. Both of us (look, looks) forward to the warm summer weather.

6. Winter (bring, brings) snow and ice, so activity outdoors (is, are) more difficult.

7. On snowy days, cross-country skiing and walking (is, are) our only options.

B. **Read each sentence. If there is an error in subject-verb agreement, write the correct verb form in the blank. If the sentence is correct as written, write *Correct*.**

8. The women living in the upstairs apartment are sisters.

   _____

9. At the other end of the first floor is two brothers.

   _____

10. These four elderly people spends lots of time together.

    _____

11. Where does they get their energy?

    _____

12. There is lots of community activities to keep them active.

    _____

13. In the building lobby is a bulletin board posting events and news.

    _____

14. The class appealing to most residents are a computer Internet course.

    _____

To check your answers, see page 188.

GED Essay: Choose the Best Word, pages 116–117

A. **Think about each word below. What words might be used in place of it? Write two or three choices. Use a thesaurus or dictionary if you like.**

1. look

   _____   _____   _____

2. walk

   _____   _____   _____

3. good

   _____   _____   _____

4. bad

   _____   _____   _____

B. **The paragraphs below use weak, repetitive words. Revise each paragraph, using better word choices.**

1. Harold is a good worker. He is at work on time. He is nice to the people he
   works with. When the job gets harder, Harold does not complain or quit. He just
   works harder. His coworkers like Harold. They like working with him.

   _____

   _____

   _____

   _____

2. The restaurant we went to last week was great. The room was nice, and the
   service was good. But of course the best part was the food. The roast beef was
   good, and so was the fish. My friend and I both had good chocolate desserts. I
   would go back to that restaurant any time.

   _____

   _____

   _____

   _____

To check your answers, see page 188.

Spell Well, pages 122–125

Use the homonym chart on page 122 if you need help.

A. Cross out the incorrectly spelled word in each sentence below. Write the correct spelling above it.

1. Every person should right his or her name on the sign-in sheet.

2. They're are two different entrances to the fair.

3. Its important that each child registers at either the front or side door.

4. The fair sponsors want know child to leave without a toy and balloon.

5. When the volunteers need a brake, they can ask for some backup help.

6. Last year, the Lions Club through a similar fair in our community.

7. In the passed, we've been able to entertain over 300 children.

8. Whose in charge next year?

9. Their is always a need for more volunteers and donations.

10. We'd love too be able to serve more children.

B. Write a complete sentence using each word below.

11. threw

_____

12. too

_____

13. they're

_____

14. its

_____

15. affect

_____

To check your answers, see page 188.

Punctuation, pages 126–129

A. Insert correct punctuation in the following sentences. If a punctuation mark is misused, cross it out.

1. Why do people so often not tell the truth

2. Even our leaders seem to lie more than they used to

3. My friends, and I try to be as honest as possible with each other

4. Lying cheating and stealing are all forms of dishonesty and disrespect

5. Whenever my girlfriend lies I tell her she is not respecting me

6. The truth may be difficult to tell but lies get you in trouble down the road

7. One lie can easily lead to another, if you are not careful

8. It is possible to tell the truth, and to do it kindly and gently

B. Use complete sentences to answer the following questions. Pay attention to correct punctuation.

9. What are the three qualities you are most proud of in yourself?

   _____

10. Name two things you did yesterday. (Use the word **I** twice.)

    _____

11. Why are you working to improve your writing skills? (Use the word **because,** and be sure your sentence is a complete one.)

    _____

12. Compare yourself to a friend. (Use the word **and** in your sentence.)

    _____

13. Contrast yourself with a friend. (Use the word **but** in your sentence.)

    _____

14. What would you do if you won a million dollars? (Use the word **if** in your sentence.)

    _____

To check your answers, see page 189.

Capitalization, pages 130–133

A. Correct the errors in capitalization in the sentences below. Draw three lines under each lowercase letter that should be a capital. Draw a line through each capital letter that should be lowercase.

1. The man who started this business is Jorge's Father.

2. Mr. Lupo opened his store in 1988 and named it anthony's fine jewelry.

3. The first shop stood at the corner of baker street and seventh avenue.

4. Soon the store outgrew the building, so the Owners decided to move.

5. In the new space on First Avenue, Mr. Lupo specialized in italian gold.

6. He made Bracelets, Charms, and Rings of 18-carat and 24-carat gold.

7. As the business grew, my uncle ralph decided to invest as well.

8. Jewelry became only one of the Products sold at the store.

9. Now Anthony and Ralph also sell goods like portuguese pottery and rugs from tibet.

10. Their store, the gift emporium, currently grosses half a million dollars every year.

B. Write complete sentences in answer to the questions below. Be sure to capitalize correctly.

11. What street do you live on, and what city and state do you live in?

    _____

12. From what country or countries did your ancestors come?

    _____

13. What are (or were) your parents' occupations?

    _____

14. When is your birthday?

    _____

15. Who is the governor of your state?

    _____

To check your answers, see page 189.

GED Essay Test: Edit Your Essay for Errors, pages 136–137

A. Edit the essay below. Correct 14 errors in grammar, spelling, punctuation, and capitalization.

The most difficult time in my life so far was the period of time, right after my mother died. I was very close with my mother and I had trouble adjusting to the fact that she was gone. In addition, they're was a lot of work to do in her house following her death. I look back on that year and am amazed at how I survived.

Because my mother was sick for so long. I was spending part of almost every day with her. I enjoyed hearing her stories of her childhood and mine during those long stretches of afternoon when she was feeling strong and alert. I also found great comfort in being the one who helped her with her medication fed her hot soup and held her when she was in enormous pain. When she died I felt like I had lost my closest companion.

After my mother's death, it become clear that her house would have to be sold. It was my responsibility to give valuables and sentimental items to relatives. I also had to hold yard sales to empty the house of it's furniture, and odds and ends. My job that april was to find a real estate agent and get the house ready to sell. By the time the year was over I was exhausted and depressed.

Today neither my family nor my friends believes how well I handled the death of my mother. I now look back at this period of my life with sadness but with pride two. I handled a difficult situation well.

B. Edit the paragraphs you wrote on page 151 and revised on page 155.

To check your answers, see page 189.

Writing Posttest

Part 1: Directions

This posttest will help you find out how much you've learned from the programs and this workbook. The questions are similar to the ones on the GED Language Arts, Writing Test. This test has 25 questions based on passages of real-life writing, just like the GED Test and the practice exercises in this book.

Here's a sample question. Read the sentence in **bold** type. Does it contain an error? If so, which option is the best way to correct the error?

A job interview creates an important <u>impression, be</u> on time.

Which is the best way to write the underlined portion of this sentence? If the original is the best way, choose option (1).

(1) impression, be
(2) impression be
(3) impression and be
(4) impression, so be
(5) impression so be

Look at the answer sheet sample, then go over the explanation of why the correct answer is correct.

Did you notice that the original sentence contains a comma splice? It has two complete sentences joined only by a comma. There is usually more than one way to fix an error like that. However, there will be only one correct answer choice for each test question. Your job is to figure out which answer choice makes the sentence correct.

You can eliminate choice (1) because the original sentence is wrong. You can also eliminate choice (2) because it would form a run-on sentence. Choices (3) and (5) are incorrect also. Each has a needed conjunction (*and* or *so*) but no comma. Choice (4) is correct because it has a comma *and* a conjunction.

Some sentences in test items are correct. If you think there is no error in a sentence or paragraph, you may be right. Some questions, such as the one above, say, "If the original is the best way, choose option (1)." Another type of question gives you this option: (5) "no correction is necessary." Look at all the choices before you decide.

As you answer the questions, fill in the grid on page 165. (You will use a similar answer sheet when you take the GED Test.) When you are finished, check your answers on page 176. On the chart on page 177, circle the items you answered correctly. The chart will help you figure out whether you should review any material in this workbook.

Directions

1. Read the sample test item on page 164 to become familiar with the test format.

2. Take the test on pages 166 through 175. Read each passage and then choose the best answer to each question.

3. Record your answers on the answer sheet below, using a No. 2 pencil.

4. Check your work against the Answers and Explanations on page 176.

5. Enter your scores in the evaluation chart on page 177.

WRITING POSTTEST ■ ANSWER SHEET

Name _____   Date _____

Class _____

1. ①②③④⑤	6. ①②③④⑤	11. ①②③④⑤	16. ①②③④⑤	21. ①②③④⑤
2. ①②③④⑤	7. ①②③④⑤	12. ①②③④⑤	17. ①②③④⑤	22. ①②③④⑤
3. ①②③④⑤	8. ①②③④⑤	13. ①②③④⑤	18. ①②③④⑤	23. ①②③④⑤
4. ①②③④⑤	9. ①②③④⑤	14. ①②③④⑤	19. ①②③④⑤	24. ①②③④⑤
5. ①②③④⑤	10. ①②③④⑤	15. ①②③④⑤	20. ①②③④⑤	25. ①②③④⑤

Choose the <u>one best answer</u> to each question.

<u>Questions 1 through 6</u> are based on the following e-mail message.

From: judyq@planetlink.net

Date: Tuesday, January 12

To: storemanager@leons.com

Subject: Unsafe parking lot

(A)

(1) I am writing to tell you about a dangerous situation at your store. (2) Snow piled very high at the northeast corner of your parking lot. (3) A driver pulling out cannot see over the snow pile to check for traffic.

(B)

(4) I pulled out of your parking lot this afternoon to head south on Nagle Avenue, I could not see the traffic coming toward me. (5) I had to pull into the traffic lane in order to see around the snow pile I was nearly hit by a truck. (6) Since Nagle is such a narrow street I barely had room to swing out of the way.

(C)

(7) Please contact your plowing contractor immediately. (8) To have this situation taken care of. (9) The snow pile must be moved back away from the street. (10) You would not want anyone to be hurt in an accident on your property. (11) Say an accident did take place. (12) Then your parking lot could be blocked off for several hours. (13) Your landscaping could be damaged as well. (14) As you can see, making the parking lot safe is just good business!

A loyal customer,

Judy Quinch

1. Sentence 2: **<u>Snow piled</u> very high at the northeast corner of your parking lot.**

   Which is the best way to write the underlined portion of this sentence? If the original is the best way, choose option (1).
   (1) Snow piled
   (2) Snow, piled
   (3) Snow is piled
   (4) Snow piling
   (5) Snow pile

2. Sentence 4: **I pulled out of your parking lot this afternoon to head south on Nagle Avenue, I could not see the traffic coming toward me.**

   Which correction should be made to sentence 4?
   (1) insert <u>When</u> at the beginning
   (2) insert <u>Because</u> at the beginning
   (3) insert a comma after <u>afternoon</u>
   (4) remove the comma after <u>Avenue</u>
   (5) no correction is necessary

3. Sentence 5: **I had to pull into the traffic lane in order to see around the snow pile I was nearly hit by a truck.**

Which is the best way to write the underlined portion of this sentence? If the original is the best way, choose option (1).

(1) pile I
(2) pile, I
(3) pile, after
(4) pile and
(5) pile, and

4. Sentence 6: **Since Nagle is such a narrow street I barely had room to swing out of the way.**

Which correction should be made to sentence 6?

(1) replace Since with So
(2) insert a comma after street
(3) insert and after street
(4) insert a comma after room
(5) no correction is necessary

5. Sentences 7 and 8: **Please contact your plowing contractor immediately. To have this situation taken care of.**

Which is the best way to write the underlined portion of these sentences? If the original is the best way, choose option (1).

(1) immediately. To have
(2) immediately to have
(3) immediately as if to have
(4) immediately having
(5) immediately, and to have

6. Sentences 11 and 12: **Say an accident did take place. Then your parking lot could be blocked off for several hours.**

The most effective combination of sentences 11 and 12 would begin with which group of words?

(1) If an accident did take place, your
(2) Say an accident in your parking lot
(3) By taking place in your parking lot,
(4) An accident, if taking place,
(5) Blocked by an accident, your

Questions 7 through 13 are based on the following announcement.

The New Public Library— More Services for You

(A)

(1) Riverdale's new public library offers many services. (2) Of course, the library still had a wonderful collection of books. (3) However, a town like ours needs many resources to support learning, creativity, and community activity. (4) You and all your family are invited to come and attend free classes, book discussions, and story hours.

(B)

(5) Riverdale Library, like most modern libraries, offer many services through the Internet. (6) Patrons can access the Internet and e-mail. (7) Many patrons use the library catalog through our website, and some of the library's databases are online also. (8) These services have brung our library into the 21st century.

(C)

(9) There is several community rooms in which Riverdale residents can hold meetings. (10) Would your book group like to hold their meeting at the library? (11) Also, the program coordinator has contacts with local speakers and is available to help residents. (12) You and her can work together to put on a special program for your group. (13) The library even provides refreshments!

7. Sentence 2: **Of course, the library still <u>had</u> a wonderful collection of books.**

Which is the best way to write the underlined portion of this sentence? If the original is the best way, choose option (1).
   (1) had
   (2) having
   (3) was having
   (4) has
   (5) have

8. Sentence 4: **You and all your family are invited to come and attend free classes, book discussions, and story hours.**

Which correction should be made to sentence 4?
   (1) change <u>are</u> to <u>is</u>
   (2) change <u>are</u> to <u>been</u>
   (3) insert a comma after <u>come</u>
   (4) replace <u>attend</u> with <u>be attending</u>
   (5) no correction is necessary

9. Sentence 5: **Riverdale Library, like most modern libraries, <u>offer</u> many services through the Internet.**

Which is the best way to write the underlined portion of this sentence? If the original is the best way, choose option (1).

(1) offer
(2) offered
(3) offering
(4) have offered
(5) offers

10. Sentence 8: **These services <u>have brung</u> our library into the 21st century.**

Which is the best way to write the underlined portion of this sentence? If the original is the best way, choose option (1).

(1) have brung
(2) have brought
(3) brung
(4) has brought
(5) bringing

11. Sentence 9: **There is several community rooms in which Riverdale residents can hold meetings.**

Which correction should be made to sentence 9?

(1) replace <u>There</u> with <u>They</u>
(2) change <u>is</u> to <u>are</u>
(3) change <u>is</u> to <u>will be</u>
(4) replace <u>can hold</u> with <u>held</u>
(5) no correction is necessary

12. Sentence 10: **Would your book group like to hold their meeting at the library?**

Which correction should be made to sentence 10?

(1) replace <u>your</u> with <u>one's</u>
(2) change <u>like</u> to <u>have liked</u>
(3) replace <u>their</u> with <u>its</u>
(4) insert a comma after <u>meeting</u>
(5) no correction is necessary

13. Sentence 12: **You and her can work together to put on a special program for your group.**

Which correction should be made to sentence 12?

(1) replace <u>her</u> with <u>she</u>
(2) replace <u>her</u> with <u>hers</u>
(3) change <u>can work</u> to <u>have worked</u>
(4) change <u>put</u> to <u>be putting</u>
(5) no correction is necessary

Questions 14 through 19 are based on the following newsletter article.

Build a Community at Work— Organize a Lunch-Break Group!

(A)

(1) A lunch-break group is an informal gathering during the lunch hour. (2) Employees can organize a lunch-break group around any topic of interest. (3) Whether your a receptionist or a vice president, everyone is welcome in a lunch-break group.

(B)

(4) If you want to start a lunch-break group talk to Martha Riley in the front office. (5) You can count on Ms. Riley if you need to publicize your group. (6) She will ask you to name your group set a date, and reserve a meeting place.

(C)

(7) Lunch-break groups can be about serious topics, but there often just for fun. (8) One group is called All My Employees, and it's members are soap opera fans who watch together every Friday! (9) Last Fall, the Fantasy Football group tracked its teams on a huge board in the break room. (10) We also have a group for parents with young children. (11) Think now about what type of lunch-break group you'd like to join.

14. Sentence 3: **Whether your a receptionist or a vice president, everyone is welcome in a lunch-break group.**

Which correction should be made to sentence 3?
- **(1)** replace your with you're
- **(2)** insert a comma after receptionist
- **(3)** change vice president to Vice President
- **(4)** remove the comma after president
- **(5)** no correction is necessary

15. Sentence 4: **If you want to start a lunch-break group talk to Martha Riley in the front office.**

Which correction should be made to sentence 4?
- **(1)** change want to wanted
- **(2)** insert a comma after start
- **(3)** insert a comma after group
- **(4)** insert a comma after Riley
- **(5)** change front office to Front Office

16. Sentence 6: **She will ask you to name your group set a date, and reserve a meeting place.**

Which correction should be made to sentence 6?
(1) insert a comma after <u>you</u>
(2) replace <u>to</u> with <u>too</u>
(3) replace <u>your</u> with <u>you're</u>
(4) insert a comma after <u>group</u>
(5) remove the comma after <u>date</u>

17. Sentence 7: **Lunch-break groups can be about serious topics, but there often just for fun.**

Which correction should be made to sentence 7?
(1) remove the comma after <u>topics</u>
(2) remove the word <u>but</u>
(3) replace <u>there</u> with <u>they're</u>
(4) replace <u>there</u> with <u>their</u>
(5) replace <u>for</u> with <u>four</u>

18. Sentence 8: **One group is called All My Employees, and it's members are soap opera fans who watch together every Friday!**

Which correction should be made to sentence 8?
(1) remove the comma after <u>Employees</u>
(2) replace <u>it's</u> with <u>its</u>
(3) change <u>soap opera</u> to <u>Soap Opera</u>
(4) insert a comma after <u>fans</u>
(5) change <u>Friday</u> to <u>friday</u>

19. Sentence 9: **Last Fall, the Fantasy Football group tracked its teams on a huge board in the break room.**

Which correction should be made to sentence 9?
(1) change <u>Fall</u> to <u>fall</u>
(2) replace <u>its</u> with <u>it's</u>
(3) insert a comma after <u>teams</u>
(4) replace <u>board</u> with <u>bored</u>
(5) no correction is necessary

Questions 20 through 22 are based on the following article.

Two Good Ways to Learn a Skill

(A)

(1) What's the best way to learn a new skill? (2) It depends on what your learning style is. (3) You might be the kind of person who needs to try things out for yourself. (4) On the other hand, you might want somebody to show you how first. (5) If you know how you learn best, you can save yourself a lot of frustration. (6) Some people learn best through trial and error. (7) Are you the kind of person who likes to just dive in and try something new? (8) If you don't mind making mistakes, you might be this kind of "trial-and-error learner." (9) Such a person is usually too impatient to read directions or watch a demonstration.

(B)

(10) Do you like to learn the right way to do something first? (11) If you like to have a guide to follow, you are probably a "procedure learner." (12) Some procedure learners learn well from reading directions. (13) That's why reading skills are important. (14) Others learn better if they are shown by someone else.

20. Which revision would improve the effectiveness of paragraph A?

Begin a new paragraph with
(1) sentence 2
(2) sentence 4
(3) sentence 5
(4) sentence 6
(5) sentence 8

21. Which sentence would be most effective if inserted at the beginning of paragraph B?

(1) On the other hand, some people like to learn the steps of a procedure in order.
(2) A counselor or teacher can help you figure out your learning style.
(3) You really need to figure out what type of learner you are.
(4) Learning styles can change over your lifetime.
(5) Always have someone show you a new skill before you try it on your own.

22. Which revision would improve the effectiveness of paragraph B?

(1) remove sentence 10
(2) remove sentence 11
(3) remove sentence 12
(4) remove sentence 13
(5) remove sentence 14

Questions 23 through 25 are based on the following article.

Don't Talk to Strangers? Not Always!

(A)

(1) Children are usually taught not to talk to strangers. (2) However, this advice is too simple. (3) Children need to know *which* strangers they *should* talk to when they need help. (4) They also have to memorize their home phone number.

(B)

(5) For example, take Sammy, who is six years old. (6) Suppose Sammy gets separated from his older brother in the supermarket.

(C)

(7) Sammy needs help from an adult, but all the adults nearby are strangers. (8) He needs to find the right kind of stranger to help him.

(D)

(9) First, teach children to ask for help from adults wearing uniforms or name badges. (10) Second, when you take children out in public, show them where they should go if they need help.

23. Which revision would improve the effectiveness of paragraph A?
    (1) remove sentence 1
    (2) remove sentence 2
    (3) remove sentence 3
    (4) remove sentence 4
    (5) no revision is necessary

24. Which revision would improve the effectiveness of the article?
    (1) join paragraphs A and B
    (2) remove paragraph B
    (3) join paragraphs B and C
    (4) join paragraphs C and D
    (5) no revision is necessary

25. Which sentence would be most effective if inserted at the beginning of paragraph D?
    (1) Obviously, Sammy should go to the front of the store.
    (2) Children can't tell the difference between a store worker and a customer.
    (3) Strangers are not always dangerous.
    (4) Safety is important in many different types of situations.
    (5) Here are two simple strategies to help kids find the right kind of stranger.

Answers and explanations are on page 176.

Part 2: Directions

Read the writing topic in the box. Use the steps outlined below it to write an essay about the topic. Then evaluate your work using the guidelines on page 177.

Use everything you have learned in the programs and in this workbook to write an essay for this posttest writing assignment.

> TOPIC
>
> Think of one thing you would like to do before your life is over.
>
> In an essay, identify the thing you would like to do and explain why. Use your personal experience, observations, and knowledge to support your essay.

Step 1: Come Up with Ideas

Take a few minutes to think about the topic. Jot down your ideas below or on another sheet of paper. Make a cluster or a brainstormed list, or use any other method that works for you.

Study your ideas. What will be the main point of your essay? Write a thesis statement here:

Thesis statement: _____

_____

Now go back and evaluate your ideas. Cross out ones that don't support your thesis. Add new ones if you think of them.

Step 2: Organize

Look again at your ideas. On a separate sheet of paper, group related ideas and label them. Create an outline, a picture, a chart, or other organizer. Show what each paragraph will be about.

Step 3: Write a Draft

Now turn your organized ideas into an essay. Start with your thesis statement. Work from your outline, picture, or other organizer. Turn your ideas into sentences. Turn your groups of ideas into paragraphs. Turn *off* that critic voice in your head, and let the writer voice come through loud and clear. Don't forget to include an introduction and a conclusion.

Step 4: Revise Your Essay

Take some time to review your essay. Read it carefully. Read for content: Is your thesis clear? Is there enough support? Read for organization: Are ideas in order? Are all ideas relevant?

Do major revisions first, then minor revisions.

Step 5: Edit Your Essay

Check your word choice, grammar, spelling, punctuation, and capitalization. Check especially for your own target errors.

Now copy your essay onto a clean sheet of paper. Make all the revision and editing changes. Make this essay your best work possible.

Evaluation guidelines are on page 177.

Posttest Answers and Explanations

1. **(3) Snow is piled** Sentence 2 is a fragment because it does not have a complete verb. Choice (3) makes a complete sentence by completing the verb.

2. **(1) insert When at the beginning** Sentence 4 is a comma splice. The dependent conjunction *When* makes it a complex sentence with the introductory thought at the beginning.

3. **(5) pile, and** Sentence 5 is a run-on. Adding a comma and a FANBOYS conjunction makes it a correct compound sentence.

4. **(2) insert a comma after street** Sentence 6 is a complex sentence, and the dependent clause comes first. Therefore, a comma is needed after it.

5. **(2) immediately to have** Sentence 8 is a fragment. It only needs to be attached to the previous sentence.

6. **(1) If an accident did take place, your** This option makes sentence 11 a dependent clause. It also combines the two thoughts into one smooth complex sentence that shows the relationship between them: *If an accident did take place, your parking lot could be blocked off for several hours.*

7. **(4) has** You need to change the past-tense verb *had* to the present tense *has* because the passage as a whole is in the present tense.

8. **(5) no correction is necessary** The sentence is correct as written.

9. **(5) offers** The subject of the sentence is singular, *Riverdale Library.* The phrase set off by commas, *like most modern libraries,* should be ignored when choosing the verb.

10. **(2) have brought** The past-participle form of the irregular verb *bring* is *brought.*

11. **(2) change is to are** The subject of the sentence is plural (*rooms*). The sentence is in inverted order. When you see *There* at the beginning of a sentence, look for the subject after the verb.

12. **(3) replace their with its** The antecedent of the pronoun is *group,* which names a collection of individuals. It is a singular noun, so it requires the singular pronoun.

13. **(1) replace her with she** You need a subject pronoun in this sentence: *you and she.*

14. **(1) replace your with you're** Test the sentence by reading it aloud with *you are* in place of *your.* It makes sense that way, so the contraction must be correct.

15. **(3) insert a comma after group** You need a comma after the introductory dependent clause *If you want to start a lunch-break group.*

16. **(4) insert a comma after group** This sentence contains a series of three phrases: *name your group, set a date,* and *reserve a meeting place.*

17. **(3) replace there with they're** Substitute the two words that make up the contraction, and you will see that it is correct in the sentence: . . . *but they are often just for fun.*

18. **(2) replace it's with its** Substitute the two words that make up the contraction, and you can see that the possessive, not the contraction, is correct in this sentence.

19. **(1) change Fall to fall** Seasons are not capitalized.

20. **(4) sentence 6** The main idea switches at sentence 6. Paragraph A has too much in it. It both introduces the topic of the article and describes one learning style.

21. **(1) On the other hand, some people like to learn the steps of a procedure in order.** This sentence makes a good topic sentence for paragraph B. It introduces the second type of learning style.

22. **(4) remove sentence 13** The idea of reading skills does not relate directly to the topic of the article.

23. **(4) remove sentence 4** Sentence 4 may discuss a good idea, but it's not directly related to the topic of the article.

24. **(3) join paragraphs B and C** These two paragraphs are very closely related. They both describe the same example situation, so they should be combined.

25. **(5) Here are two simple strategies to help kids find the right kind of stranger.** This sentence is a good topic sentence for paragraph D. It introduces the two ideas in the paragraph, telling the reader what to expect.

Posttest Evaluation

PART 1 DIRECTIONS: Check your answers on page 176. On the chart below, circle the numbers of the questions you got correct. In the last column, write the total number you got correct in each section. If you got more than 2 wrong in any section, review the programs and workbook pages listed.

Questions	Total Correct	Program
1, 2, 3, 4, 5, 6	___ / 6 correct	4: Effective Sentences Pages 80–99
7, 8, 9, 10, 11, 12, 13	___ / 7 correct	5: Grammar and Usage Pages 100–119
14, 15, 16, 17, 18, 19	___ / 6 correct	6: Spelling, Punctuation, and Capitalization Pages 120–139
20, 21, 22, 23, 24, 25	___ / 6 correct	3: Organized Writing Pages 60–79

PART 2 DIRECTIONS: Use the questions below to evaluate your writing sample. If possible, show your writing to a teacher, coworker, or fellow student for feedback.

1. Does your essay address the topic? Did you set up a focus and stick to it?

❏ yes ❏ no

*Comments:*_____

2. Is the essay well organized, with an overall flow of ideas for the reader?

❏ yes ❏ no

*Comments:*_____

3. Is the essay divided into paragraphs? Does each paragraph stick to its own topic?

❏ yes ❏ no

*Comments:*_____

4. Have you included interesting details that make the writing come alive?

❏ yes ❏ no

*Comments:*_____

5. Are the sentences clear and correct? When you read the essay out loud, does it read well?

❏ yes ❏ no

*Comments:*_____

Answers and Explanations

PROGRAM I
GETTING IDEAS ON PAPER

Practice I (page 23)

Did you write without stopping for five minutes? If so, great. It's all right if your free writing is messy or doesn't always stick to the point. If you were not able to write without stopping for five minutes, try again.

Practice 2 (page 25)

Did you fill up the page with your thoughts? If so, great. If not, try again.

Practice 3 (page 27)

1. Did you fill in the names of two readers, along with three topics that would interest each?

2–3. Model personal letter:

It still seems strange to be in another state, many miles away from you. I'm not used to it yet. I miss being near you all.

My apartment is working out OK. Cesare and Pete are good guys, and we have fun. They are working on the construction site too, so we share rides and go out together after work.

I don't know if I will stay here after this job is done. I should have enough money to get home, but I might not be able to find a job at home. Let me know if you hear of anything at the plant.

Practice 4 (page 29)

1–2. Check each letter to see if you included these elements:
- ❑ your address
- ❑ today's date (month, day, and year)
- ❑ a greeting at the top of the letter, like this: *Dear Melinda,*
- ❑ a closing at the end of the letter, like this: *Your friend, Love,* or *Sincerely,*
- ❑ your signature

3. Model e-mail message:

> **Subject:** Movie
> Dave:
> Do you want to go to the movie with me Saturday night? That new horror film is playing. It starts at 7:30. I could pick you up. Let me know.
> Jay

Practice 5 (page 31)

1. You should have written details about the time and place of your event—the time of day, the season, where it happened, what the place looked like.

2. Did you write details about the people in your story? Who are they, how old are they, what do they look like?

3. Did you write the events of your story? Did you number them in sequence? Did you pick out one moment that is especially important?

Practice 6 (page 33)

Use this checklist to review your story:
- ❑ Did you set the stage by describing the time and place and introducing the people?
- ❑ Did you describe the action in sequence, using interesting details?
- ❑ Did you tell the reader why the story matters?

Using the Writer's Tool (page 35)

Did you write for at least ten minutes in your journal? If not, try again.

GED Essay Practice (page 37)

1. Possible details include taking exercise classes, running, taking long walks, gardening, practicing yoga.

2. Possible details include eating or drinking too much, getting angry, blaming other people for their problems.

GED Writing Review (pages 38–39)

A. Possible details:
1. Sometimes when I think I should really be nice, it's hard to be honest.
2. Telling the truth has gotten me in trouble, like when I told the boss something he didn't want to hear.
3. It would be better if we could be more honest about our feelings instead of pretending not to feel anything all the time.

B. 4. Possible details:
   a. If you tell the truth, you never have to remember anything. I found out that every lie I tell just waits around to trip me up later.
   b. Lies have hurt my family a lot. My brother lied to my parents over and over about what he was into in high school— and now he's in jail.
   c. I think honesty would help our government. However, if politicians told the truth, probably nobody would ever vote!

C. Review your letter.
- ❑ Does it help your friend see and hear the event?
- ❑ Does it show what your emotions were, from beginning to end?
- ❑ Does it follow the form of a letter, with address, date, greeting, and closing?

PROGRAM 2
THE WRITING PROCESS

Practice 1 (page 43)

Remember that in brainstorming, there are no wrong answers. The goal is to let your ideas flow onto the paper. Don't stop to think about whether they are good ideas. Were you able to do that? If not, you might want to practice a few more minutes of brainstorming about the topic.

Practice 2 (page 45)

Did making a cluster help free up your mind to find new ideas? Some people take to clustering right away, but not everybody. If it did not work for you this time, keep an open mind. Try it again another day on another topic.

Practice 3 (page 47)

1. Did you write a thesis statement that states your main point about the person you are writing about?
2. Make sure all the ideas you have left truly relate to the thesis statement.
3. Did you come up with at least two groups of ideas about the person you are writing about? Did you label each group to show how those ideas support the thesis?
4. You should have created a picture for your writing about a person.
   - ❑ Does your plan show the thesis statement?
   - ❑ Did you create groups of supporting ideas?

Practice 4 (page 49)

1. Did you write a thesis statement that states your discussing about the goal you are discussing?
2. Make sure all the ideas you have left truly relate to the thesis statement.
3. Did you come up with two or more supporting ideas related to your thesis? Did you write details under each supporting idea?
4. Were you able to let your writer voice take over as you wrote your first draft? Did you make your inner critic take a day off? If you had a hard time hearing your writer voice, don't get discouraged. More writing practice will help!

   Here is Dorothy's first draft of her story about her father:

   My father's life was hard, but I remember him with love. My father was a hardworking miner. He was very muscular because he did heavy work all his life. He never could get completely clean because of the coal dust.

   My father always argued with my mother. She wanted to move away from the mining town. He wanted to stay with what he knew. I think he understood why my mother wanted to go away. However, he could not bring himself to take the risk to start a new life.

   My father played with my brothers and me sometimes. He did not relax or have fun with friends, though. He seemed sad a lot of the time, and he did not show a lot of affection. But when he looked at us gently, we could see that he loved us.

Practice 5 (page 51)

A. 1. Did you check to see if—
   - ❑ you have a clear thesis statement?
   - ❑ you might be able to add more good ideas?
   - ❑ all your ideas relate to the thesis?
   2. Did you check to see that—
   - ❑ the order of your ideas makes sense?
   - ❑ all the ideas in each paragraph belong?
   - ❑ you might create more paragraphs?

   You might not have filled in every line. Maybe you are satisfied with some aspects of your writing already!

B. Did you follow your plan for revising your writing? If not, did you find a better way as you went along? If you had trouble revising your writing, you may find it helpful to talk about the writing with a teacher or a friend. Be sure to take notes as you talk.

Practice 6 (page 53)

Did you follow the three-step editing strategy? Did you add any errors to your Target Error List? If you had trouble editing your writing, continue to work with a teacher or friend.

GED Essay Practice (page 57)

1. Why is <u>so-and-so</u> a <u>hero</u> to me?
2. If you had problems brainstorming ideas about the person you chose, try clustering. You should come up with at least four or five good ideas.
3. Check to see that your thesis statement answers the question "Why is so-and-so a hero to me?" If it does, you are responding to the essay topic.

GED Writing Review (pages 58–59)

A. 1. These ideas should be crossed out:
   cable has many different kinds of channels
   sometimes tape soap operas
   Kenny wants me to watch sports with him
   too much football on TV for me
   2. The remaining ideas fit into the three categories.
   TV Shows Educate
   learn from history programs
   learn from Biography channel
   learn from science programs
   watch GED prep programs on public TV

TV Shows Help Relax

TV comedies can be good for relaxing
and relieving stress

enjoy watching cartoons with my son
and laughing

TV Shows Inspire

watch movies like <u>Glory</u> based on
inspiring stories

Olympic Games and athletes inspire me

B. **1.** Did you cross out ideas that don't
belong? Did you add any new ideas?

2. Did you organize your ideas by grouping
them and labeling the groups? Your
labels should show how the ideas
support your thesis.

3. Does your picture show your thesis
statement? Does it show the groups of
ideas that support it?

C. Be sure you used the Writing Process in the
Handbook to write, revise, and edit
your essay. Then ask your teacher or a
friend to read your essay.

PROGRAM 3
ORGANIZED WRITING

Practice 1 (page 63)

A. Here are the paragraphs that needed topic
sentences. Your topic sentences may be
somewhat different. Do your topic sentences
clearly lead the reader into the paragraph? Do
they signal shifts in time?

Finally, we arrive at the ballpark. People
are streaming along all the sidewalks. We find
the right gate, then we manage to find our seats.
We settle in and argue about who will go get hot
dogs.

**Eventually, we notice that the game has
started.** Frank Bellini hits a home run, his first
time up at bat! The crowd goes wild. It's a good
game. We forget about the hot dogs and root for
our team.

**Then in the seventh inning, the game gets
really exciting.** The Stars are ahead. But the
Stars pitcher walks two batters in a row. Sox
fans are screaming. The next batter is Loren
Malteez. He hits a double, brings in one run.
Now the score is tied.

B. Does your topic sentence sum up the ideas you
listed about your Sunday afternoon? Would it
lead into a paragraph written about them?

Practice 2 (page 65)

A. Below is a new topic sentence. With this
sentence, the second sentence would need to be
revised a bit as well. Your topic sentence may be
somewhat different. Is it specific enough to
introduce the paragraph for the reader?

**My friend Anna learned that only she is
responsible for her credit card bill.**

B. Here are the paragraphs that needed topic
sentences. Your topic sentences may be different.
Do your topic sentences clearly lead the reader
into the paragraph? Do they signal the writer's
point of view?

Using credit cards is easy. All kinds of
businesses take credit cards. I can order over the
phone or on the Internet with my credit card. I
can even charge movie tickets and popcorn at
the refreshment counter. I almost never have to
have cash or write a check.

**The problem is that I forget how much I
have spent.** One day I buy groceries. The next
day it's new shoes and shin guards so my
daughter can play soccer. Then I need a new bus
pass to get to work. By the end of one week, I
don't even remember all the things we paid for
with our card.

C. Make sure your topic sentence covers the point
you would make about your Sunday afternoon.

Practice 3 (page 67)

A. Here's how you should have marked Cortney's
paragraphs. You should have circled the words
or phrases in **bold**.

<u>Every cooking class follows the same pattern.</u>
The teacher starts with a demonstration of a
cooking skill, like making pastry. ~~Light pastry is
very hard to make.~~ **Then** we study a recipe
together, and we talk about planning the steps in
the recipe. **Next,** we prepare by getting out the
ingredients and tools we need. **Finally,** we work
in teams to make the dish. The teacher checks
each team's work at the end.

<u>Last week,</u> I learned a big lesson about
<u>cakes.</u> **At first,** I didn't understand why we were
supposed to beat the batter for so long. **Then** I
saw the difference in the cakes. The team next to
us had this perfect, light cake. **But** ours was kind
of flat and tough. **When** the teacher came
around, she said we didn't beat enough air into
the batter.

B. Use this checklist to review your paragraph:
- ❑ Do you have a specific topic sentence
  that leads the reader into your paragraph?
- ❑ Does your paragraph stick to one idea?
  Should any sentences be crossed out?
- ❑ Did you use transitions to signal the flow of
  ideas?

Practice 4 (page 69)

Use this checklist to review your paragraphs:
- ❑ Do you have a specific topic sentence
  that leads your reader into your paragraph?
- ❑ Does your paragraph stick to one idea?
  Should any sentences be crossed out?
- ❑ Did you use transitions to signal the flow of
  ideas?

Practice 5 (page 71)

A. Here is a possible revision of the original paragraph. (Yours will probably be different.)

Most people remember their first job. Like a lot of people, I got my first job in fast food. It paid minimum wage. It was fun at first. But after a while, I saw that every shift was the same. It was not an exciting job, and it never would be.

<u>The best thing about the job was that some of the other workers were pretty interesting.</u> One of the managers had gone to school for many years, and he could speak Russian. I'll never know how he ended up managing a burger joint. There were other talented people too. Theresa was too good at math to spend her career counting out four pickle slices per burger. John talked about all the books he read and how he was writing a mystery novel.

At the time, I couldn't understand why these people stayed in their jobs. But that was 25 years ago, and I'm wiser now. I know that there are lots of problems that hold people back. Being "smart" isn't important. You have to have a certain drive. You can't be afraid of hard work or of a challenge. It helps to have support from your family and friends to make something out of your life. And you have to stay out of trouble.

Practice 6 (page 73)

A. Here is a possible revision of the original paragraphs. (Yours may be a little different.) An added topic sentence is underlined.

Many people think that working at home is easy. But when I got a job stuffing envelopes at home, it was not easy for me.

I thought I wanted to work at home. I could set my own hours. I would not have to take the bus to work. I would also save money on work clothes and lunches.

<u>However, there were problems I did not predict.</u> I did not have a good place to work in the apartment. It was hard to put in enough hours. My family distracted me. My boss told me that I had to produce more. Otherwise, he would have to let me go. Then he fired me.

At first I was very angry with myself. Yet I did learn something from the experience. I got a job in a supermarket, and I love taking the bus every day!

Using the Writer's Tool (page 75)

A. Sample pros of cell phones: can be reached in an emergency; can call someone in an emergency; don't have to search out a public phone; can keep in touch with loved ones no matter where you are. Sample cons: people use when driving—cause accidents; people talk too loudly on them in public; rings can be annoying; can run up big phone bills

B. Here are sample ideas for a Venn diagram comparing a person as a child and today, as an adult:

In the left circle: shy; a little afraid of new things, of trying; picked on by big sister
In the right circle: more outgoing; more willing to take chances; stand up to sister (occasionally)
In the overlapping middle area: love horses; feel most comfortable outdoors

GED Essay Practice (page 77)

A. Use this checklist to review your introduction.
- ❑ Did you state your topic clearly?
- ❑ Did you include a thesis statement that tells the main point of your writing?
- ❑ Did you include a hook—a fact, idea, or question that will get the attention of your reader?

GED Writing Review (pages 78–79)

A. 1. b. Antonya needs a new first paragraph to introduce her essay. As is, no paragraph introduces the topic or thesis statement of the essay.

    2. b. Paragraphs B and C should be combined into one paragraph. Both paragraphs relate to the same main idea.

    3. b. Paragraph D should be divided into paragraphs. The sixth sentence begins a new main idea.

    4. a. Antonya should write a conclusion for her essay. As is, no paragraph restates the main point or gives the reader something to think about.

B. Review your planning:
- ❑ Did you list reasons that nature is important in the first column and reasons it is not important in the second?
- ❑ Did you outline, draw a picture, or use some method to plan your essay?

C. Use this checklist to review your essay.
- ❑ Does your introduction restate the topic and tell the thesis of your essay?
- ❑ Does the conclusion restate the thesis and leave your reader something to think about?
- ❑ Does each body paragraph have a specific topic sentence to lead the reader into the paragraph?
- ❑ Does each body paragraph develop just one supporting idea with several interesting details?
- ❑ Do transition words help your reader follow the flow of ideas?

PROGRAM 4
EFFECTIVE SENTENCES

Practice 1 (page 83)

A.
1. C
2. C
3. F
4. F
5. C

B. Here are some sample answers. Yours may be different.

2. To get there, we will be riding all night long.
3. Drivers from all over the country will be racing.
4. We certainly will be tired at the end of the day.

C. (3) **Marissa is ready** This answer completes the fragment by supplying the missing subject and verb: *Marissa is ready for a night on the town.*

Practice 2 (page 85)

A.
1. F
2. F
3. F
4. C
5. F

B. The bold words show where the fragments were attached to other sentences.

I am a driver for a commercial laundry. I deliver clean linens and **uniforms to** hotels and restaurants on my route. I also pick up all the dirty laundry from the customers. It's hard work. When new customers meet **me, they** are sometimes very surprised. They expect a truck driver to be a big guy. I'm a woman, and I weigh about a hundred pounds. I like being **strong and** working hard.

C. (4) **report, we ask** This answer correctly attaches the fragment to the sentence: *If you must make a police report, we ask that you contact the district office first.*

Practice 3 (page 87)

A. Sentences 1 and 3 are correct compound sentences.

B. Here are sample answers. Yours may be different.

1. Laura's wedding dress didn't fit her daughter, **so** Nikki saved up for a new one.
2. I can't swim, **but** I can run faster than anyone.
3. He works in the warehouse, **and** she works in the front office. OR He works in the warehouse, **but** she works in the front office.
4. You can pay now, **or** you can pay later.
5. Make sure your sentence has two complete thoughts connected with a comma and a FANBOYS conjunction.

C. (5) **no correction is necessary** The sentence is a correct compound sentence.

Practice 4 (page 89)

A.
1. ✓
2. RO
3. ✓
4. CS
5. RO

B. You might have chosen different conjunctions in some sentences.

1. Ricky paid the phone bill, **but** he forgot to pay the cable company.
2. There are trees down everywhere, **and** our electricity is out.
3. Correct
4. The gas company has a new payment plan, **and** we might try it for a year.
5. The plumber cut off all the water, **so** you can't take a shower.

C. (2) **insert and after the comma** This answer corrects the comma splice by supplying a conjunction: *Marina is our PR aide, and she will give you a tour of the new building.*

Practice 5 (page 91)

A. Sentences 1, 2, and 5 are complex sentences.

B. You might have chosen different conjunctions. Be sure you placed commas correctly

2. **Although** the storm had been terrible, it was a gorgeous morning.
3. Some friends called for help **because** their roof was torn off.
4. **As** TV crews roamed the trailer park, residents stared at their ruined homes.
5. Many families will live in local hotels **until** their homes are repaired.
6–7. Make sure your complex sentences have a main clause and a dependent clause. Make sure you put a comma after the dependent clause when it is at the beginning of the sentence.

C. (1) **replace Many with Because many** This answer corrects a comma splice by changing the first complete thought into a dependent clause: *Because many workers were affected by the storm, we will operate the plant on short shifts today.*

Practice 6 (page 93)

A.
1. **b.** New workers must fill out forms before they can be paid.
2. **a.** If you are not a U.S. citizen, you must show a green card.

B. Here are some sample answers. Yours may be different.

1. If you get to know people on your shift, you will be able to ask them questions. OR Get to know people on your shift so that you will be able to ask them questions.

2. Martin will join your shift on Friday after he has finished his training.

3. Nadia is an expert operator, and she trains people to use the grinder.

4. You must follow the safety rules, or else you could get hurt.

C. **(3) quickly since they** This answer turns two short choppy sentences into one smooth complex sentence: *The new workers will learn quickly since they are a smart group.*

Using the Writer's Tool (page 95)

A. Here are sample answers. Yours may be different. Did you use an opening phrase?

2. On the plane at last, we breathed a sigh of relief.

3. Walking down the ramp, we could see his folks waving at us.

B. Here are sample answers. Yours may be different. Did you use an ending phrase?

1. I think it's wonderful being a tourist, exploring a new place all day long.

2. Moe loves to walk through strange cities, looking at the people and the buildings.

3. Laurel visits art museums, drinking in paintings with her eyes.

C. Here are sample answers. Yours may be different. Did you use a renaming phrase?

1. Laurel, a painter, has taken many art classes.

2. Laurel helped Rafael, her best student, learn to paint landscapes.

GED Essay Practice (page 97)

A. Here are sample answers. Yours will be different. Read your answers aloud and with feeling. Do your sentences have interesting variety?

1. When Kyle hurt his ankle at the softball game and couldn't stand on it, we took him to the emergency room.

2. Kyle's X ray showed a broken ankle. The doctor, an orthopedist, gave him a splint.

3. With the Velcro straps, Kyle can take the splint on and off to shower.

B. Review your writing:
- ❑ Did you combine sentences to get rid of repeated words and ideas?
- ❑ Did you create a strong impact with at least one short sentence?
- ❑ Did you create at least one long, flowing sentence?

C. Read your essay out loud. Use feeling and emphasis. Do many sentences seem to have the same general sound or shape? If so, try to vary them even more.

If your sentences have plenty of variety, you should hear a little rhythm when you read your essay aloud!

GED Writing Review (pages 98–99)

1. **(3) insert <u>and</u> after the comma** Sentence 2 is a comma splice. By inserting *and* after the comma, you supply the needed conjunction.

2. **(2) Printing, we** Sentence 3 is an unattached fragment. It needs to be connected to sentence 4. A comma must follow it because it is a dependent clause.

3. **(1) insert a comma after <u>paper</u>** The compound sentence needs a comma before the conjunction.

4. **(5) You can order** Sentence 6 is a fragment. It needs a clear subject and verb.

5. **(3) insert a comma after <u>letter</u>** Sentence 2 is a complex sentence. The dependent clause comes first, so a comma is needed.

6. **(4) work, but you** Sentence 3 is a comma splice. It needs a conjunction that makes the meaning clear.

7. **(5) no correction is necessary** The complex sentence is correct as written.

8. **(3) one, so** Sentence 9 is a fragment that can be attached to sentence 8 to make a compound sentence.

PROGRAM 5 GRAMMAR AND USAGE

Practice 1 (page 103)

A. **1.** Mr. Santiago saw the movie yesterday, and <u>he</u> enjoyed <u>it</u>. **Arrows should connect *he* with *Mr. Santiago* and *it* with *movie*.**

2. Mr. Santiago's sons recommended the movie. <u>His</u> wife could not go. **An arrow should connect *His* with *Mr. Santiago's*.**

3. A kind woman offered a man an aisle seat because <u>she</u> saw <u>he</u> needed help. **Arrows should connect *she* with *woman* and *he* with *man*.**

4. When Mr. Santiago asked some teenagers to be quiet, <u>they</u> stopped talking. **An arrow should connect *they* with *teenagers*.**

B. Here are some sample sentences.

1. It is **my** turn to wash the dishes.

2. You can dry **them**.

3. Together, **we** will get the dishes done in no time.

C. **(3) they** The plural pronoun *they* is correct because it is replacing the plural noun *pants*.

Practice 2 (page 105)

A. **1.** *Correct:* **you** *Incorrect:* **I**

2. *Correct:* **They, them** *Incorrect:* **us**

3. *Correct:* **our** *Incorrect:* **him**

B. **1.** **their** (possessive)

2. **them** (object)

3. **She** (subject)

C. **(2) replace <u>Him</u> with <u>He</u>** The subject pronoun *He* is needed in the compound subject *He and I.*

ANSWER KEY

Practice 3 (page 107)

A. 1. appeared; past
2. plans; present
3. lived; past
4. will provide; future

B. 1. owns
2. raised
3. will appear
4. hopes

C. (2) **will have** The clue word *Tomorrow* tells you that the verb should be in the future tense.

Practice 4 (page 109)

A. 1. *Incorrect:* been
2. *Correct:* wrote *Incorrect:* maked
3. *Incorrect:* seen
4. *Correct:* got, fell

B. 1. took
2. ran
3. broke; got
4. seen

C. (4) **sent** The verb *send* is irregular; the correct past-tense form is *sent.*

Practice 5 (page 111)

A. 1. *Subject:* cousin and brother
Verb: attends, NA
2. *Subject:* They *Verb:* like, A
3. *Subject:* class *Verb:* are studying, NA
4. *Subject:* mother or mother-in-law
Verb: sit, NA
5. *Subject:* child and school
Verb: make, A

B. 1. make
2. help
3. eat
4. is
5. improve
6. seems

C. (2) change <u>arrive</u> to <u>arrives</u> Because the singular *mail* is the nearest subject to the verb, the correct verb form is *arrives,* not *arrive.*

Practice 6 (page 113)

A. 1. *Subject:* announcements *Verb:* is, NA
2. *Subject:* people *Verb:* help, A
3. *Subject:* volunteers *Verb:* comes, NA
4. *Subject:* time *Verb:* is, A
5. *Subject:* donations *Verb:* is, NA

B. 1. feel
2. is
3. goes
4. are
5. is

C. (3) change <u>sign</u> to <u>signs</u> The single subject *supervisor* needs the verb *signs*, not *sign*. Watch out for the interrupting phrase *from short-distance trips.*

GED Essay Practice (page 117)

1. Here is a sample rewrite. Your word choice may be different.

    Another quality that good leaders possess is courage. Strong, effective leaders not only have the courage to say what they believe, but they also stand behind what they say. They don't waver.

2. Ask a peer to edit your paragraph and comment on your choice of words.

GED Writing Review (pages 118–119)

1. (2) **change <u>is</u> to <u>are</u>** The subject of the sentence is plural—*fees*. Therefore, the correct verb form is *are*, not *is*.

2. (4) **change <u>took</u> to <u>will take</u>** The correct tense is the future *will take*. The clue words are *within the month*.

3. (3) **he or she** The pronouns are subjects of a dependent clause beginning with *unless*. Therefore, the subject pronouns *he* and *she* are needed.

4. (5) **expect** The subject is plural: *you and your family*.

5. (3) **change <u>is</u> to <u>are</u>** Don't be confused by the inverted order of this sentence. The subject of the sentence is plural: *ways*. Therefore, the verb *are* is correct.

6. (3) **replace <u>your</u> with <u>their</u>** The antecedent of the pronoun is *owners*. In this sentence, the writer is discussing people who own computers in general, not the just the reader.

7. (2) **has introduced** The subject is the business *New Tech Company*, which is singular. Therefore, *has introduced* is the correct verb form, not *have introduced*.

8. (5) **is** The verb must agree with the subject closest to it, which is *program*, a singular noun. Therefore, *is* is the correct choice.

PROGRAM 6
SPELLING, PUNCTUATION, AND CAPITALIZATION

Practice 1 (page 123)

A. 1. Your idea for speeding up work is **new**, but it is two weeks too late.
2. When the shift is **through**, we'll meet here in the break room.
3. There are **four** new workers on our shift.
4. Go through the two double doors, **past** the office, and then turn right.

B. Here are some sample sentences.
1. I am going to accept that new job.
2. All of my family except my brother came to the party.
3. The weather can affect how you're feeling.
4. What effect does the weather have on you today?

C. **(4) replace <u>threw</u> with <u>through</u>** The homonym *through* is the correct choice; *threw* is the past tense of *throw*, a verb, which does not make sense here.

Practice 2 (page 125)

A. 1. The decrepit old house was on **its** last legs.
2. The owners put the house on the market because **they're** moving south.
3. The **neighbors** are wondering who's going to buy such a dismal home.
4. If **you're** handy with a hammer and nail, this house is a buyer's bargain.
5. **It's** a shame the home's owners did not maintain it.

B. Here are some sample sentences.
1. If the children don't come in soon, **they're** not going to get to watch TV tonight.
2. People should be more friendly with **their** neighbors.
3. Please put the bags down over **there**.

C. **(3) replace <u>they're</u> with <u>their</u>** The homonym *their* is the correct choice because it shows possession; *they're* is the contraction meaning *they are*.

Practice 3 (page 127)

A. 1. Yay! Matt scored a perfect 300! (A period would also be correct after the sentence.)
2. A winning bowler needs good form**,** a strong wrist**,** and confidence.
3. You also need to practice, practice, and practice some more.
4. Matt, Luis, and Rey started bowling when they were teens.
5. Where should we go to celebrate**?**

B. Here are some sample sentences.
1. My three favorite foods are avocados, pasta, and ice cream.
2. Why did you want to be president of the United States?
3. I care most about Eddie, Anna, Jack, and Maggie.

C. **(2) insert a comma after <u>listening</u>** A comma is needed to separate the items in the series *listening, reading, and talking.*

Practice 4 (page 129)

A. 1. Dealing with difficult customers is a skill, and many people are not good at it.
2. Whenever a training session on this topic is held, all employees must attend.
3. **Correct** as written
4. Because our store values customer satisfaction, employees should respond to all complaints quickly and respectfully.

5. By talking politely and calmly, you can soothe most angry customers.

B. Here are some sample sentences.
1. We'll eat at home tonight, or we'll get Chinese takeout.
2. I was planning on making spaghetti, but I forgot to buy the sauce.
3. I'll drive to the restaurant even though it's only a block away.
4. While you are waiting, can you set the table?

C. **(2) remove the comma after <u>manager</u>** A comma is usually not needed when the independent clause (*You can always transfer a call to your manager*) comes first in the sentence.

Practice 5 (page 131)

A. 1. **Asking** your employer for direct deposit of your paycheck is a great idea.
2. My employer, the **Healthy Pet Food Company**, deposits my check into my checking account.
3. On **Friday I** record the deposit in my checkbook.
4. I live in **Boston, Massachusetts,** and the taxes alone here require me to be as careful as possible with my money.
5. Remember that the **Boston Tea Party** was all about taxes too!

B. Here are some sample sentences.
1. I was born in Dearborn, Michigan.
2. The name of the place I work is Sweet Life Plastics Factory.
3. My favorite toothpaste is Crest.
4. I'm a big fan of the Detroit Tigers.
5. I really like to shop at Target.

C. **(5) no correction is necessary** The sentence is correct as written. All the words are capitalized correctly.

Practice 6 (page 133)

A. 1. Believe it or not, going to an **art gallery** can be stress-relieving and relaxing.
2. Many museums in **cities** are open late on **Thursdays** for people who work weekdays.
3. In fact, there is often no **entry fee** if you arrive after six o'clock in the **evening**.
4. For a relaxing visit, don't try to see every single painting by a master **artist** like **Picasso**.
5. The museum I enjoy most in the **world** is in **Washington, D.C.,** and is called the **National Museum of African Art**.

B. Here are some sample sentences.
1. My favorite museum is the Frick in New York City.

ANSWER KEY

2. I enjoy playing cards, watching motocross, and listening to music.

3. One of my favorite family members is Enrique, my cousin.

4. I don't like Mondays, but I love summer.

C. (4) **change** <u>Team</u> **to** <u>team</u> The noun *team* should not be capitalized here because it is not a specific name.

GED Essay Practice (page 137)

    While people like my Uncle Dave seem to [be] blessed with good luck, other people seem to have nothing but bad luck. My sister, for example, has had a rough life. Last year [was] is extremely tough on her. She was in a car accident. [that] It was no fault of hers. Her teeth were knocked loose, but even worse her eyes were damaged. Several months later she was eating at a fast-food restaurant, and got food poisoning. [She] Ended up in the hospital for a [week] weak. All this happened after she lost her job in that same factory that my Uncle had worked in.

GED Writing Review (pages 138–139)

1. (4) **change** <u>hillside medical center</u> **to** <u>Hillside Medical Center</u> *Hillside Medical Center* names a specific place and should be capitalized.

2. (5) **change** <u>apple's</u> **to** <u>apples</u> The plural form *apples* is correct, not the singular possessive *apple's*.

3. (2) **fiber, vitamins, and minerals** A comma is needed between the nouns in the series.

4. (4) **remove the comma after** <u>levels</u> There is no need for a comma after levels; *protect against lung and colon cancer* is not an independent clause.

5. (1) **replace** <u>excepted</u> **with** <u>accepted</u> The homonym *excepted* is incorrect; *accepted* means to receive or take, which makes more sense in this sentence.

6. (3) **insert a comma after** <u>children</u> A comma is needed after *children* because the dependent clause *Even though Felicia is almost a year younger than these two children* comes first in the sentence.

7. (1) **replace** <u>they're</u> **with** <u>there</u> The homonym *they're* is not correct because the words *they are* do not make sense here. The homonym *there* does.

8. (2) **change** <u>Classroom</u> **to** <u>classroom</u> The word *classroom* should not be capitalized because it is not part of a title of a specific place.

EXTRA PRACTICE

Free Writing, page 140

A. Did you write nonstop for the whole five minutes? Remember that you should not have made corrections.

B. Your answer should contain many different ideas about having a lot of money. No spelling, grammar, or punctuation corrections are necessary.

Letters and E-Mail, page 141

A. Your letter should include your address and the date.

B. Be sure that your e-mail message includes both an e-mail address (real or made-up) and a subject.

Personal Stories, page 142

A. You should have included ideas for the three ages you chose from the time line. You may have written about a childhood memory or a more recent event in your life.

B. Your story should have set the stage for the event, described exactly what happened, and then ended with a look back.

GED Essay: Development and Details, page 143

A. Here are some possible details you might have added. Your details should include examples of teamwork in each situation, reasons that support or explain its importance in the situation, and specific information that helps a reader picture teamwork in that situation.

   1. One person can do the grocery shopping while another is responsible for cleaning.

   2. On a construction site, you can always see one person operating a crane or bulldozer while another directs him from the ground.

   3. In a good marriage, spouses let each other know what is working in the family and what is not.

B. Your writing should include details and ideas that make the concept of teamwork easily understood by a reader.

Brainstorm and Cluster, page 144

A. In the first box, your ideas should relate to the topic of renting an apartment (for example, find good location, know how to negotiate with landlord, or pain in the neck). In the second box, be sure your ideas relate to world peace.

B. Your cluster should consist of circles filled with ideas about growing old that are connected to that circle or to each other.

Outline, page 145

A. Thesis: Credit cards have both advantages and disadvantages.

   Supporting Idea 1: Some positive things about credit cards

a. good because safer than carrying cash

b. helpful when ordering over the phone

c. can use easily to order online

d. can help you keep track of purchases

Supporting Idea 2: Some negative things about credit cards

a. too easy to make impulse purchases

b. finance charges can be ridiculously high

c. my brother is over $10,000 in debt on his card

d. many people misuse them, get into financial trouble

e. some credit card companies take advantage

B. There are several possible ways to group the ideas. Sample outline:

Thesis: Different kinds of pets have different advantages.

Supporting idea 1: Dogs make good pets for some people.

a. dogs are affectionate and loyal

b. dogs love to lie at your feet or in your lap

c. dogs require training, walking outside

Supporting idea 2: Cats make good pets for other people.

a. cats are more independent—great for people not home a lot

b. cats don't require as much attention or time

Supporting idea 3: Snakes make good pets too.

a. snakes easy to care for, stay in confined area

b. snakes are fascinating

Revise and Edit, page 146

A–B. Ask your instructor or a friend to review your work and help you decide if you revised and edited it appropriately.

GED Essay: Respond to the Topic, page 147

A. 1. no 2. yes 3. yes 4. no

B. The quality you wrote should be important in order to get a job done. Some possibilities include perseverance, teamwork, loyalty, determination, energy. Make sure your thesis statement answers the topic question.

Topic Sentences, page 148

A. 1. b 2. c 3. a

B. Your topic sentence should be similar to this one: "It is important for me to be honest with my friends, my family, and my coworkers."

Organized Paragraphs, page 149

A–B. Be sure each paragraph you wrote follows the organization plan clearly and uses appropriate transition words.

Divide and Combine Paragraphs, page 150

A. The four paragraphs should begin with these four sentences:

There are two ways to get a job done well.

If you decide to get the job done by yourself, you do not have to depend on other people.

If you decide to get people to help you with the job, there are entirely different advantages and disadvantages.

These two methods for getting a job done well can both work.

B. The four paragraphs should begin with these four sentences:

The procedures for opening the shop are outlined below.

Your first priority is store entrance.

Your next focus should be on set-up.

Next, start the food preparation.

GED Essay: Write an Introduction and Conclusion, page 151

A. Your introduction should:

- have a clear topic
- have a thesis statement that tells the main point

B. Your conclusion should:

- restate your thesis
- leave your reader with something to think about

Complete Sentences, page 152

A. 1. C 2. F 3. C 4. F 5. F 6. C

B. My job as a childcare assistant has a lot going for it. First of all, kids are neat to work **with, even though** they sometimes exhaust you completely. The hours are excellent if you have school-age children of your own. Also, every day **brings** new surprises. The children are always growing, and every week they become someone new. It's nice to see immediately the fruits of your labors. Unfortunately, on the down side **is** the pay. Living on minimum wage is neither easy nor fair. The quality of care children receive will **improve when** our pay increases to reflect its true value.

Compound Sentences, page 153

A. 1. Time is running short, **so** live life to the fullest.

2. We wanted to buy a house, **but** we can afford only to rent right now.

3. Sam will have a cheeseburger, **and** Natalie wants a chicken sandwich.

4. Eat, drink, and be merry, **for** tomorrow we may die.

5. You can finish the dishes tonight, **or** you can leave them until the morning.

B. Your answers should include:

- a comma
- a FANBOYS conjunction
- another complete thought

ANSWER KEY

Complex Sentences, page 154

A. Sample answers:
1. He will not receive a raise this year if his work does not improve.
2. Because my son is quite tall for his age, the basketball coach wants him to try out.
3. I almost always eat dessert after I finish my dinner.
4. Unless you have a better idea, we'll go to the movies tonight.
5. The mice will play while the cat's away.

B. For 6, 7, and 10, your answers should include a comma and an independent clause.
For 8, 9, and 11, your answers should include a dependent clause beginning with a dependent conjunction.

GED Essay: Vary Sentence Structure, page 155

A. You should have combined some sentences, divided some sentences, and added phrases to vary the structure in each paragraph.

B. Did you combine sentences to make compound or complex sentences? Add a short sentence? Ask a question?

Nouns and Pronouns, page 156

A. 1. Underlined nouns: forecaster, snow, night, midnight
   Circled pronoun: it (antecedent→snow)
2. Underlined nouns: Mrs. Ortega, books, gift, granddaughter, copy, *Pat the Bunny*
   Circled pronouns: your (antecedent→ Mrs. Ortega), I, you (antecedent→Mrs. Ortega), her (antecedent→ granddaughter)
3. Underlined nouns: apples, crate, table
   Circled pronoun: them (antecedent→apples)
4. Underlined nouns: partner, vacation, year
   Circled pronouns: his (antecedent→ partner), mine
5. Underlined nouns: artist, watercolors, work
   Circled pronouns: his (antecedent→artist), he (antecedent→artist), they (antecedent→watercolors), his (antecedent→artist)
6. Underlined nouns: teenager, parents, car
   Circled pronouns: his (antecedent→teenager), they (antecedent→parents), him (antecedent→teenager)

B. 7. me
8. He
9. our
10. they
11. us
12. me
13. I

Verb Tense, page 157

A. 1. reported
2. was
3. thought
4. was
5. began; worked
6. was
7. spends
8. will take

B. 9. brought
10. chose
11. were
12. thought
13. given
14. taken

Subject-Verb Agreement, page 158

A. 1. girlfriend and I; agree
2. Hiking, biking, and skating; are
3. she or I; decide
4. situation; one; arises; stays
5. Both; look
6. winter; activity brings; is
7. skiing and walking; are

B. 8. Correct
9. At the other end of the first floor **are** two brothers.
10. These four elderly people **spend** lots of time together.
11. Where **do** they get their energy?
12. There **are** lots of community activities to keep them active.
13. Correct
14. The class appealing to most residents **is** a computer Internet course.

GED Essay: Choose the Best Word, page 159

A. Here are some possible word choices:
1. gaze, glare, inspect
2. plod, saunter, limp
3. fine, satisfying, inspirational
4. evil, malicious, rotten

B. Your rewritten paragraphs should:
- not be repetitive
- use a variety of words
- have plenty of detailed language

Spell Well, page 160

A. 1. write
2. There
3. It's
4. no
5. break
6. threw
7. past
8. Who's
9. There
10. to

B. Here are some example sentences.

11. He **threw** the trash away each night.

12. My friend will come to the movie **too**.

13. My parents say **they're** feeling old.

14. The dog wagged **its** tail whenever a guest arrived.

15. How will the job layoff **affect** you?

Punctuation, page 161

A. 1. Why do people so often not tell the truth**?**

2. Even our leaders seem to lie more than they used to**.**

3. My friends [no comma here] and I try to be as honest as possible with each other**.**

4. Lying, cheating, and stealing are all forms of dishonesty and disrespect**.**

5. Whenever my girlfriend lies, I tell her she is not respecting me as a person**.**

6. The truth may be difficult to tell, but lies get you in trouble down the road**.**

7. One lie can easily lead to another [no comma here] if you are not careful**.**

8. It is possible to tell the truth [no comma here] and to do it kindly and gently**.**

B. Be sure you included commas:
- in a series
- before a conjunction joining two independent clauses
- after a beginning dependent clause

Capitalization, page 162

A. 1. The man who started this business is **J**orge's **f**ather.

2. **M**r. **L**upo opened his store in 1988 and named it **A**nthony's **F**ine **J**ewelry.

3. The first shop stood at the corner of **B**aker **S**treet and **S**eventh **A**venue.

4. Soon the store outgrew the building, so the **o**wners decided to move.

5. In the new space on First Avenue, **M**r. **L**upo specialized in **I**talian gold.

6. He made **b**racelets, **c**harms, and **r**ings of 18-carat and 24-carat gold.

7. As the business grew, my **U**ncle **R**alph decided to invest as well.

8. Jewelry became only one of the **p**roducts sold at the store.

9. Now Anthony and Ralph also sell goods like **P**ortuguese pottery and rugs from **T**ibet.

10. Their store, the **G**ift **E**mporium, currently grosses half a million dollars every year.

B. You should have capitalized:
- proper nouns
- the first letter of the first word of a sentence
- the pronoun *I*
- words derived from proper nouns

GED Essay Test: Edit Your Essay for Errors, page 163

A. Corrections are in **bold**:

The most difficult time in my life so far was the period of time [**no comma needed**] right after my mother died. I was very close with my mother, and I had trouble adjusting to the fact that she was gone. In addition, **there** was a lot of work to do in her house following her death. I look back on that year and am amazed at how I survived.

Because my mother was sick for so long, I was spending part of almost every day with her. I enjoyed hearing her stories of her childhood and mine during those long stretches of afternoon when she was feeling strong and alert. I also found great comfort in being the one who helped her with her medication, fed her hot soup, and held her when she was in enormous pain. When she died, I felt like I had lost my closest companion.

After my mother's death, it **became** clear that her house would have to be sold. It was my responsibility to give valuables and sentimental items to relatives. I also had to hold yard sales to empty the house of **its** furniture [**no comma needed**] and odds and ends. My job that **April** was to find a real estate agent and get the house ready to sell. By the time the year was over, I was exhausted and depressed.

Today neither my family nor my friends **believe** how well I handled the death of my mother. I now look back at this period of my life with sadness but with pride **too**. I handled a difficult situation well.

B. Use the Editing Checklist on page 191 to make sure you have edited your essay for each item on the list.

Writing Handbook

The Writing Process

Come Up with Ideas
Identify your purpose.
Brainstorm or cluster.
Determine your main point—write your thesis.
Evaluate your ideas—cross out and add.

Organize Your Ideas
Group related ideas and label them.
Create an outline, a picture, a chart, or other organizer.

Write a Draft
Start with your thesis statement.
Work from an outline, picture, or other organizer of ideas.
Turn ideas into sentences.
Turn groups of ideas into paragraphs.
Turn off the "critic" voice in your head.

Revise
Let writing sit for a bit.
Read for content—Is thesis clear? Is there enough support?
Read for organization—Are ideas in order? Are all ideas relevant?
Do major revisions first, then minor revisions.

Edit
Check word choice, grammar, spelling, punctuation, capitalization.
Pay special attention to your target errors.

A finished piece of writing!

Revising Checklist

As you read, ask yourself these questions:

- Is my thesis stated clearly?
- Is there enough support for my thesis?
- Have I divided up my supporting ideas and details in paragraphs?
- Does each paragraph have a clear topic and supporting sentences?
- Is each paragraph "bite-sized"—that is, not too much to read all at once?
- Are the ideas in a clear, logical order?
- Are all the ideas relevant—does each support the main point?
- Did I use a variety of short and long sentences, as well as different sentence structures?
- Do I have an introduction?
- Do I have a conclusion?

Editing Checklist

Check for the types of errors you have studied in this book:

- Fragments
- Comma splices and run-ons
- Pronouns and pronoun agreement
- Verb forms and tenses
- Subject-verb agreement
- Commas
- Spelling
- Capitalization

Check for the errors you make most often. (See your Target Error List, page 53.)

Editing Marks

Below are marks you can use to help you revise and edit your writing.
See how they are used in the paragraph below.

- a caret (∧) to add words
- a neat cross-out to delete words
- a paragraph mark (¶) to show a new paragraph
- an arrow to move text
- three lines below a letter to capitalize it
- a slanted line through a capital letter to lowercase it

Our choir director taught us a new song. It's based on poems by the African-american poet Gwendolyn Brooks. The composer set Brooks's poems to music. The poems were about life in the ghetto. ¶ The sopranos and tenors sing the poems. The altos and basses sing sounds like a bass and drum.

GED Essay Scoring Guide

Here is the part of the GED Essay Scoring Guide that describes a high-scoring essay.

Score of 4
Effective

Reader understands and easily follows the writer's expression of ideas.

Response to the prompt (the topic in the essay assignment)	Presents a clearly focused main idea that addresses the prompt.
Organization	Establishes a clear and logical organization.
Development and Details	Achieves coherent development with specific and relevant details and examples.

Use the Revising Checklist (p. 191) to help you score high in these areas.

Conventions of Edited American English (EAE) (grammar and usage, spelling, punctuation, capitalization)	Consistently controls sentence structure and the conventions of EAE.
Word Choice	Exhibits varied and precise word choice.

Use the Editing Checklist (p. 191) to help you score high in these areas.

Reprinted with permission of the GED Testing Service. © 2001, GEDTS.